UNDERSTANDING
ESOPs

2014 UPDATE

UNDERSTANDING
ESOPs

2014 UPDATE

COREY ROSEN
SCOTT RODRICK

The National Center for Employee Ownership
Oakland, California

This publication is designed to provide accurate and authoritative information in regard to the subject matter covered. It is sold with the understanding that the publisher is not engaged in rendering legal, accounting, or other professional service. If legal advice or other expert assistance is required, the services of a competent professional person should be sought.

Legal, accounting, and other rules affecting business often change. Before making decisions based on the information you find here or in any publication from any publisher, you should ascertain what changes might have occurred and what changes might be forthcoming. The NCEO's Web site (including the members-only area) and newsletter for members provide regular updates on these changes. If you have any questions or concerns about a particular issue, check with your professional advisor or, if you are an NCEO member, call or email us.

Understanding ESOPs

Corey Rosen and Scott Rodrick

Book design by Scott Rodrick

First published in 2008; reprinted in 2013 with updates; reprinted again in 2014 with further updates.

Print ISBN: 978-1-932924-47-3
Ebook ISBN: 978-1-932924-79-4

The National Center for Employee Ownership
1736 Franklin Street, 8th Floor
Oakland, CA 94612
Phone (510) 208-1300; fax (510) 272-9510
Web site: www.nceo.org

Contents

Preface

When the National Center for Employee Ownership (NCEO) was founded in 1981, employee ownership was a relatively unknown and somewhat suspect notion. Today, we estimate that approximately 28 million Americans own stock in their companies through one kind of plan or another. Over 13 million of these employees are participants in an employee stock ownership plan (ESOP), the subject of this book.

Understanding ESOPs grew out of *The ESOP Reader*, NCEO's most venerable publication and one that goes back to the NCEO's founding in 1981. In its various incarnations, the *Reader* served as a nontechnical reference on the subject for decades. Nowadays, we at the NCEO provide a wide variety of ESOP publications (and other information resources, online and offline), and our aim in producing this new book is to present the topic in a more streamlined and efficient way so that the reader gets the depth he or she needs on certain topics, while other matters that need not be discussed in an introductory work are quickly passed over.

The first chapter of this book presents an overview of what ESOPs are, how they work, and what they are used for. Subsequent chapters delve into important topics that deserve more detailed treatment. Finally, the last chapter discusses how an ESOP can improve corporate performance and how that is linked to creating an ownership culture.

This book is for the reader who desires a comprehensive overview of the subject. There are many other issues, however, and beyond that there are other equity plans that can be used in addition to or instead of an ESOP. For more information on technical matters, communicating to employees, creating an ownership culture, and using other equity plans, see our books and informational resources.

2014 Update

This book was originally published in 2008 and revised for the 2013 printing. For the 2014 printing, the authors made minor updates throughout the book as needed.

CHAPTER I

An Overview of How ESOPs Work

Corey Rosen

An employee stock ownership plan (ESOP) is a specific way to share ownership with employees that can provide tax benefits to the company, to sellers of stock to an ESOP, and to employees. Given statutory authority in 1974 under the Employee Retirement Income Security Act (ERISA), ESOPs are governed by many of the same rules that cover 401(k) plans, deferred profit sharing plans, pension plans, and other retirement plans. Unlike these other plans, however, only ESOPs are designed to invest primarily in the stock of the employer, and only ESOPs can borrow money. ESOPs should not be confused with employee stock option plans, which are covered by a very different set of rules. Nor are ESOPs to be confused with stock purchase plans. In fact, ESOPs are almost always funded by the company, not by employee contributions.

The basic concept of an ESOP is simple. A company sets up a trust fund to acquire and hold company stock. The company can contribute shares directly, contribute cash to buy shares, or have the trust borrow money to buy stock, with the company repaying the loan through contributions to the plan. The company also can contribute cash to the trust or pay dividends or distributions on shares held by the trust. The shares, and any other contributions, are allocated to employee accounts based on an equitable formula. Companies cannot, however, make allocations based on discretionary approaches, such as performance assessments. Employees acquire vesting rights to these allocations over time. After employees terminate, their account balances are distributed to them, with some exceptions described below. The plan is governed by a trustee, usually appointed by the company's board of directors; the minimum allowable governance rights for employees are very limited, although some companies provide more extensive ones. Within broad limits, contributions to the plan are tax-deductible. Employees pay no tax on what is in their accounts until they actually receive a distribution, and even then they can roll the distribution into an IRA or other retirement plan. Some sellers to an ESOP can defer capital gains taxes on the sale, and the profits attributable to the ESOP in an S corporation are not taxable at the federal and, usually, state levels.

ESOPs are used for many reasons. The most common is to provide a vehicle for the company to fund the purchase of an owner's shares on a pretax basis, but ESOPs are also used simply to provide an additional benefit, to acquire other companies, to spin off subsidiaries or divisions, and to finance capital growth. For all their many benefits, ESOPs are not right for every company. They are more complex than other retirement plans, they do not allow as much flexibility as less tax-favored approaches to sharing ownership, and they usually are a poor fit for extremely small companies (typically under 10 to 15 employees) and companies that either are not or do not soon anticipate making a profit.

This book is written for people thinking about ESOPs. It walks you through the various rules and applications, discusses what to think about in setting up a plan, and provides guidance on how to make the plan work well for your company. As an introduction to the topic, it is not meant to be comprehensive. The NCEO does, however, have a variety of detailed publications on ESOP applications, tax issues, administrative practices, and ownership culture. For a list, go to our Web site at www.nceo.org.

This chapter provides a broad overview of ESOPs. Subsequent chapters look at ESOP applications and rules in more detail, while a final chapter discusses what may be the most important potential benefit of an ESOP, namely the potential to create a more engaged and productive culture.

The Development of ESOPs

Back in the 1950s, Louis Kelso, an investment banker and attorney in San Francisco, was pondering the question of why in a country as wealthy as the U.S. so few people had much wealth. Over half the productive assets in the country were owned by just 1% of the population. Kelso was no Marxist, however. Capitalism was one of the greatest inventions in history, he believed. The problem was there were just too few capitalists. And that, Kelso believed, augured poorly for the future.

Kelso believed that over the ensuing generation, returns to capital would greatly outpace returns to labor, something that had never been true in the U.S. Economists scoffed, but Kelso noted that more capital would be created in the next generation than all the prior ones combined. That growth rate would mean movement out of manufacturing jobs, which paid well even for relatively low skills, into jobs that paid less. That's just what happened. Real wages since the early 1970s have barely moved, but returns to capital have soared. The Dow Jones Average, for instance, only had three digits back then. As people felt more economically stressed, they would demand that the government help them out more by creating and expanding entitlement programs, another prediction that held true. Even so, people would find it harder to accumulate enough money to retire comfortably, especially as life expectancy grew. The government would have to either tax more or borrow more (and slow the economy) to deal with the problem. Kelso was prescient on every point.

But Kelso also had a solution. If more workers were capital owners, they would have an additional source of wealth besides what they could save from wages. Of course, workers couldn't easily become capitalists by buying stock precisely because their wages were stagnating, while their perceived consumption needs were growing, pushing savings rates down. Kelso noted that people with money could also borrow money to buy productive capital, something ordinary workers could not do. But if business owners would put up the collateral for their employees to become owners, the employees could borrow the money to buy shares in their employer. The company could then repay the loan out of future earnings. Kelso believed a combination of tax incentives, a special Federal Reserve lending rate for this kind of financing, and the promise of improved employee productivity would be enough to persuade many owners to agree to do this.

The special loan rates never came to be, but in 1974, Congress agreed to Kelso's ideas about tax benefits, incorporating them in a massive reform of retirement law known as ERISA (the Employee Retirement Income Security Act of 1974). Congress basically made a deal with employers: share ownership with employees and in return get a tax deduction for doing so. In addition, ESOPs would be allowed to borrow money to buy company stock, something no other benefit plan could do. That loan would be repaid out of tax-deductible corporate contributions, not employee purchases. Over the years, Congress sweetened that basic deal with a variety of additional tax incentives, including allowing certain sellers to ESOPs to defer capital gains tax on the sale of their stock, letting companies deduct dividends paid on ESOP shares if certain rules were met, and, ultimately, excluding from federal corporate income tax the ESOP's percentage of ownership in an S corporation, making a 100% S ESOP non-taxable. In return for all this, companies had to make sure the plans were run in a way that truly benefited employees on a broad and equitable basis.

That basic deal has led today to roughly 7,000 ESOPs, covering over 13 million employees and holding over $900 billion in assets. Of these, only about 3% are in publicly traded companies; the rest are in closely held companies. The median percentage ownership for ESOPs in public companies is about 1% to 10%. Most public companies maintain an ESOP along with other benefit plans. The median ownership percentage for private companies is about 30% to 40%, and over 4,000 companies are majority employee-owned. While the typical company has 20 to 500 employees, employees own a majority of the stock of such companies as Lifetouch (25,000 employees), Publix Super Markets (160,000 employees), and Houchens Industries (15,300 employees). About three-quarters of ESOPs in private companies are used to buy out an owner; the rest are typically used simply as employee benefit plans, sometimes in conjunction with borrowing money for capital acquisition.

Overall, providing generous tax incentives for ESOPs has been a good policy. Employees in ESOP companies have somewhat higher wages than comparable employees in comparable non-ESOP companies, but they also have about three times the company-related retirement assets. ESOP companies grow about 2% to 3% per year faster than would have been expected without an ESOP. Those that combine an ESOP with an "ownership culture" (one that emphasizes open-book management and high employee involvement in work-level decisions) grow 6% to 11% per year faster. Of course, these are averages. Some companies do incredibly well; others (such as Enron and United Airlines) are disasters.

The ESOP Proposition

As noted above, in creating an ESOP, a company sets up an employee benefit trust, which it funds by contributing cash to buy company stock, contributing shares directly, or having the trust borrow money to buy stock, with the company making contributions to the plan to enable it to repay the loan. Generally, at least all full-time employees with a year or more of service are in the plan. To assure that these rules are met, the company must appoint a trustee to act as the plan fiduciary. This can be anyone, although larger companies tend to appoint outside trust institutions, while smaller companies typically appoint managers or create ESOP trust committees. ESOPs are designed to invest primarily in the stock of the employer and can buy treasury shares, newly issued shares, or shares from exiting owners.

There is one very important point that is widely misunderstood: employees almost never contribute to the plan; instead, contributions are funded by the company as a benefit, and shares are allocated to employee accounts on a nondiscriminatory basis, much as in a profit sharing plan. It's worth repeating that: *as a rule, employees do not buy shares in an ESOP.* Over the years, we have found that many people considering an ESOP have a difficult time understanding how that can be. The answer is simple: the company funds the plan instead.

An ESOP can be used for many purposes, including the following:

- *To buy the shares of a departing owner of a closely held company.* This is the most common application. In C corporations, owners can defer tax on the gains they have made from the sale to an ESOP if the ESOP holds 30% or more of the company's stock and certain other requirements are met. Moreover, the purchase can be made in pretax corporate dollars.

- *To divest or acquire subsidiaries, buy back shares from the market, or restructure existing benefit plans by replacing current benefit contributions with a leveraged ESOP.*

- *To buy newly issued shares in the company, with the borrowed funds being used to buy new productive capital.* The company can, in effect, finance growth or acquisitions in pretax dollars while these same dollars create an employee benefit plan.

- *To simply be an employee benefit plan for companies that want to share ownership broadly.* In public companies especially, an ESOP contribution is often used as part or all of a match to employee deferrals to a 401(k) plan.

These benefits come in return for operating the plan under ERISA guidelines. Passed in 1974 in the wake of pension scandals, the law was broadly drafted to cover a variety of employee benefit plans, including health insurance, pension plans, profit sharing plans, ESOPs, retirement savings plans, cafeteria plans, and other benefits meant to provide financial security to a broad group of employees. The basic idea is straightforward: the government provides employees and employers with tax breaks if their plans provide benefits on a nondiscriminatory basis across the work force. To do that, ERISA relies on several key concepts:

- *Operate the plan for the "exclusive benefit of plan participants."* Despite how it sounds, a plan can benefit companies and other people as well, but when there is a conflict of interest, the interests of participants should prevail.

- *Govern the plan with an "eye sole" to the interests of participants.* The plan trustee is required by law to make sure the plan is operated primarily for the benefit of the people in it, not for the company or its owners. In an ESOP, this means, among other things, not overpaying for company stock.

- *Make prudent investment decisions for the plan.* Any funds in ERISA plans used for retirement should be invested in a way that a sensible, careful investor would invest them. Excess risk is discouraged, but so is parking all the money in a passbook savings account. There is a special exception for ESOPs, however. Here, ERISA not only permits but requires plans to be primarily invested in company stock, unless it is clear that that investment is in imminent danger of failing.

- *Broadly include those who work for the company and meet minimal requirements.* Generally, this means at a minimum all employees who have worked for at least 1,000 hours in a year must become eligible in the following year. There are some exceptions, however, such as employees covered by a bargaining agreement or employees in a separate line of business.[1]

- *Allocate benefits fairly.* Benefits can be allocated based on relative pay or a more level formula, but pay over $260,000 (as of 2014; this amount is indexed for inflation) does not count.

- *Make benefits subject to vesting.* Most retirement plans allow companies to require that employees stay a certain amount of time before they earn any benefits contributed by the company.

- *Have a process for employees to contest decisions.* ERISA spells out a variety of specific procedures by which employees can argue that they were improperly denied benefits. The first level is to try to resolve the matter within the company. The second is to ask the government to step in (usually the U.S. Department of Labor [DOL], although the DOL's resources for this are limited). The third is to sue in federal courts.

- *Preserve the benefit in a trust for long-term wealth building.* All retirement plans governed by ERISA provide the employee with special tax benefits. Unlike other ownership arrangements we discuss in this book, ownership through an ESOP is not taxed when the employee is vested in the benefit, but rather when it is received (which normally is some time much later, such as after the employee leaves the company). But employees usually have only a limited ability to take money out of the plan while still working (mostly in 401(k) plans through loans) and face a tax penalty if they don't put the money in an IRA or other retirement account when they actually get it after leaving the company.

In short, if you want the benefits of one of these plans, you have to meet a number of rules. You cannot pick and choose who

---

1. There are also provisions that allow a company to exclude up to 30% of its non-highly compensated employees who otherwise meet the requirements, but it is extremely rare and usually impractical for ESOP companies to use this exception.

you want to allow to be in the plan, nor can you base their awards on assessments of merit or adopt other discretionary approaches. If you can live with that, however, these plans are greatly more financially advantageous, to the company and the employee, than other approaches.

Funding

The most sophisticated use of an ESOP is to borrow money. The company borrows money from a lender and reloans it to the ESOP; the ESOP then uses the money to buy shares. The company makes tax-deductible contributions to the trust to enable it to repay the loan. This is called a "leveraged" ESOP. The company can also use dividends on the shares to repay the loan; these dividends become deductible to the company. In effect, the parallel loan structure allows the company to borrow money to acquire stock and, by funneling the loan through the ESOP, deduct both principal and interest. The company can use proceeds from the loan for any legitimate business purpose. Sellers to an ESOP can also be lenders. The stock is put into a "suspense account," from where it is released to employee accounts as the loan is repaid.

The ESOP can also be funded directly by discretionary corporate contributions of cash that are used to buy existing shares or simply by the contribution of shares. These contributions to an ESOP are tax-deductible, generally up to 25% of the total eligible payroll of plan participants.

How Shares Get to Employees

If the company contributes shares or cash to buy shares, these contributions are immediately allocated to employee accounts in the plan. In a leveraged ESOP, the acquired shares are placed in a suspense account. As the loan is repaid, a percentage of the total shares acquired is released to employee accounts in an amount equal to either the principal paid that year or the percentage of total principal plus interest due that is paid that year. The amount *contributed* to repay the principal on the loan is what counts for determining whether the company is within the limits for contributions allowed each year and for the purpose of calculating the tax deduction. The *value* of the shares released, however, is the amount used on the corporate income statement, where it counts as a compensation cost. From the employees' perspective, it is this value of shares released that will also matter to them because this is the amount they will see added to their accounts.

Companies can also use dividends or earnings distributions (in S corporations) to pay for leveraged shares. In that case, the dividends paid on the shares not yet allocated to employee accounts must release shares that have that much value to employee accounts, based either on the employees' current relative account balances or on the same formula for releasing shares paid for out of company contributions. For shares already allocated, however, the shares in the suspense account that are released must be allocated on the basis of relative account balances.

Once the shares are in the plan, the rules for ESOPs are similar to the rules for other tax-qualified ERISA plans in terms of who is a plan participant, how allocations are made, vesting, and distribution, but several special considerations apply.

At least all employees over age 21 who work for more than 1,000 hours in a plan year must be included in the next plan year (or earlier) unless they are covered by a collective bargaining unit (and the ESOP issue is negotiated in good faith) or are in a separate line of business with at least 50 employees not covered by the ESOP, or fall into one of several limited anti-discrimination exemptions. Companies can always have more liberal rules for participation.

An alternative approach provides three tests for coverage. To use this approach, a company applies percentage tests to at least a minimum employee group. This group must include all employees 21 or older who have completed at least 1,000 hours of service in a plan year, but it can exclude nonresident aliens, employees in a separate line of business with 50 or more employees, and employees covered by a collective bargaining agreement. After these exceptions have been taken, the tests can be met if:

1. At least 70% of non-highly compensated employees are covered, or

2. The percentage of non-highly compensated employees who are covered is at least 70% of the percentage of highly compensated employees covered, or

3. There is a classification system that does not discriminate in favor of highly compensated employees, and the average benefit percentage (generally, the percentage of compensation contributed to the plan) for the covered non-highly compensated group is at least 70% of that contributed to the covered highly compensated group.

Few ESOPs, however, use these alternative tests, both because they want to create a culture of ownership that is inclusive and because how much can be contributed to a plan overall is limited by the payroll of employees in the plan (meaning that a company wishing to maximize the amount the ESOP can buy will want to maximize plan participation).

Plans have one or more "entry dates" for employees once they become participants. An employee who has satisfied the plan's minimum age and service requirements must begin participation in the plan not later than the first of (1) the first day of the plan year beginning after the date on which the requirements were met or (2) the date six months after the date on which the requirements are met. Participation can begin at an earlier date, however. Many plans, for example, have entry dates every six months or every year, and employees become participants at the first entry date after requirements are met.

Shares are allocated to individual employee accounts based on relative eligible compensation. Generally, all W-2 compensation is counted, but there is leeway to define compensation differently, such as by excluding bonuses, provided that it does not favor more highly compensated individuals; on a more level formula, such as per capita, by seniority, or by placing a cap on pay that can be considered; or some combination of the two, such as one point for seniority and one for relative pay. If relative pay is not used, however, plans must be tested annually to determine whether any highly compensated individual, generally defined as someone belonging to either the top 20% by payroll in the company or those making more than $115,000 per year (as of 2014), is receiving more than what the relative pay formula would indicate. In that case, the excess must be returned to the plan and reallocated to other participants. Finally, ESOP allocations can be used as a match to employee deferrals to a 401(k) plan, in which case all or part of the allocation may be determined by how much the employee defers. This approach requires complex anti-discrimination testing for both plans. Relatively few ESOPs use this approach.

Eligible compensation includes the pay of only those employees actually participating in the plan. As noted earlier, it excludes pay over $260,000 (as of 2014). It also excludes the pay of sellers to an ESOP who take advantage of the ability to defer tax on the gains from the sale proceeds, as well as their immediate relatives, more-than-25% owners, and certain relatives of the more-than-25% owners.

The allocated shares are subject to vesting. If the plan provides for vesting all at once, called cliff vesting, employees must be 100% vested after three years of service; if vesting is gradual, it must not be slower than 20% after two years and 20% more per year until 100% is reached after six years. Plans can vest faster than these schedules. Companies do not have to provide credit for years of service before the ESOP, but many companies do. Some companies give a year of credit for every year of prior service; some give a year for every x number of years.

When employees reach age 55 and have 10 years of participation in the plan, the company must either give them the option of diversifying 25% of company stock in their account balances among at least three other investment alternatives or simply pay the amount out to the employees. At age 60 with 10 years of service, employees can have a cumulative total of 50% diversified or distributed to them.

When employees retire, die, or become disabled, the company must distribute their vested shares to them not later than the last day of the plan year following the year of their departure. For employees leaving before reaching retirement age, distribution must begin not later than the last day of the sixth plan year following their year of separation from service. Payments can be in substantially equal installments out of the trust over five years, or they can be made in a lump sum. With the installment method, a company normally pays out a portion of the stock from the trust each year.

Closely held companies and some thinly traded public companies must repurchase the shares from departing employees at their fair market value, as determined by an independent appraiser. This so-called "put option" can be exercised by the employee in one of two 60-day periods, one starting when the employee receives the distribution and the second period one year after that. The employee can choose which one to use. This obligation should be considered at the outset of the ESOP and be factored into the company's ability to repay the loan.

This repurchase obligation should be assessed on a periodic basis. There are a variety of ways to fund the obligation, including making cash contributions to the ESOP to enable it to buy back the shares, building a cash reserve, using insurance proceeds, releveraging the ESOP, and other techniques. The impact of the obligation on valuation should be calculated. Normally, the obligation will reduce future share prices somewhat if share prices are growing, making future repurchases more manageable.

Limitations on Contributions

Congress was generous in providing tax benefits for ESOPs, but there are limits. Generally, companies can contribute and deduct an amount equal to up to 25% of the total eligible payroll of plan participants, whether contributed in the form of cash or stock or in payments to fund the repayment of an ESOP loan. Eligible pay is essentially all the pay (including employee deferrals into benefit plans) of people actually in the plan up to $260,000 per participant (as of 2014; like the other dollar limits described here for defined contribution plans, this is indexed annually for inflation).

In C corporations, there are separate 25% deductibility limits for (1) contributions to pay principal on an ESOP loan (interest is deductible as it always is on a loan) and (2) additional contributions to the ESOP or to other defined contribution plans, provided they are not used to repay interest or principal on the ESOP loan. A company with a leveraged ESOP and a profit sharing plan, for example, has a 50% total deductibility limit (up to 25% for a leveraged ESOP plus up to 25% for other defined contributions not related to the loan). However, in S corporations, company contributions to a leveraged or non-leveraged ESOP and other defined contribution plans all fall under a single 25%-of-eligible-pay calculation. Interest payments on the ESOP loan are deductible as interest, but the company cannot deduct more than 25% of eligible pay to cover both the interest and principal payments.

On top of this, in C corporations, "reasonable" dividends paid on shares acquired by the ESOP can be used to repay an ESOP loan, and these are not included in the 25%-of-pay calculations. S corporations can use distributions on earnings to help repay the loan, although these are not deductible as they are in C corporations (but they are also not taxable to the ESOP). In a leveraged ESOP in a C corporation, if employees leave the company before they have a fully vested right to their shares, their forfeitures, which are allocated to everyone else, are not counted in the percentage limitations. They are counted in an S corporation ESOP, however.

There are a number of limitations to these provisions, however. First, no one ESOP participant can get a contribution of more than 100% of pay in any year from the principal payments on the loan or the direct ESOP contributions made that year that are attributable to that employee, or more than $52,000 (as of 2014), whichever is less. In figuring payroll, pay over $260,000 per year (as of 2014) does not count toward total contribution limits. Second, if there are other qualified benefit plans, these must be taken into account when assessing this limit. This means that employee deferrals into 401(k) plans, as well as other employer contributions to 401(k) plans, stock bonus, or profit sharing plans, are added to the ESOP contribution and cannot exceed 100% of pay or $52,000 (as of 2014) in any year.

Third, the interest on an ESOP loan repayment in a C corporation is excludable from the 25%-of-pay individual limit only if not more than one-third of the benefits are allocated to "highly compensated employees," as defined by Internal Revenue Code Section 414(q). If the one-third rule is not met, forfeitures are also counted in determining how much an employee is getting each year.

Voting

In private companies, employees must be able to direct the trustee as to the voting of shares *allocated* to their accounts on several key issues, including closing, sale, liquidation, recapitalization, and other issues having to do with the basic structure of the company. They do not, however, have to be able to vote for the board of directors or on other typical corporate governance issues, although companies can voluntarily provide these rights. Instead, the plan trustee votes the shares, usually at the direction of management. In public companies, employees must be able to vote on all issues.

What these rules mean is that governance is not really an issue for ESOP companies unless they want it to be. If companies want employees to have only the most limited role in corporate governance, they can; if they want to go beyond this, they can as well. In practice, companies that do provide employees with a substantial governance role find that it does not result in dramatic changes in the way the company is run.

Finally, in private companies and some thinly traded public companies, all ESOP transactions must be based on a current appraisal by an independent, outside valuation expert.

Tax Benefits to the Selling Shareholder

One of the major benefits of an ESOP for closely held C corporations is found in Section 1042 of the Internal Revenue Code. Under it, a seller to an ESOP may be able to qualify for a deferral of taxation on the gain made from the sale. Several requirements apply, the most significant of which are:

1. The seller must have held the stock for three years before the sale.

2. The stock must not have been acquired through stock options or other employee benefit plans.

3. The ESOP must own 30% or more of the value of the company's shares and must continue to hold this amount for three years unless the company is sold. Shares the company repurchases from departing employees do not count. Stock sold in a transaction that brings the ESOP to 30% of the total shares qualifies for the deferral treatment.

4. Shares qualifying for the deferral cannot be allocated to the accounts of the selling shareholder(s); to lineal descendants, brothers or sisters, spouses, or parents of the selling shareholder(s); or to any more-than-25% shareholders.

If these rules are met, the seller (or sellers) can take the proceeds from the sale and reinvest them in "qualified replacement property" during the period running from 3 months before to 12 months after the sale and defer any capital gains tax until these new investments are sold. Qualified replacement property essentially means stocks, bonds, warrants, or debentures of domestic corporations receiving not more than 25% of their income from passive investment. Mutual funds and real estate trusts do not qualify. If the replacement securities are held until death, they are subject to a step-up in basis at that time, so capital gains taxes would never be paid.

Very often, lenders ask for replacement securities as part or all of the collateral for an ESOP loan. This strategy may be beneficial to sellers selling only part of their holdings because it frees the corporation to use its assets for other borrowing and could enhance the future value of the company.

As with all transactions in closely held ESOP companies, the price the ESOP pays for the shares cannot be more than fair market value as assessed by an independent appraiser. The price is what a financial buyer would pay—someone who would operate the company as a stand-alone entity, not as part of another enterprise as a synergistic buyer might. That means an ESOP may not be able to meet the price of some synergistic buyers, although it does offer better tax benefits on the sale.

Corporate Tax Benefits

As noted above, companies can use ESOPs to borrow money and repay the loan entirely in pretax dollars. In addition, companies can take a tax deduction for reasonable dividends that are used to repay a loan, that are passed through directly to employees, or that employees voluntarily reinvest in company stock. Contributions not used to repay an ESOP loan are tax-deductible as well, even if made in the form of treasury or new shares.

ESOPs in S Corporations

ESOPs can own stock in S corporations. While these ESOPs operate under most of the same rules as they do in C corporations, there are important differences. As noted above, interest payments on S corporation ESOP loans count toward the contribution limits (they normally do not in C companies). Dividends (i.e., S corporation "distributions") paid on ESOP shares are also not deductible. Most important, sellers to an ESOP in an S corporation do not qualify for the tax-deferred Section 1042 rollover treatment.

On the other hand, the ESOP is unique among S corporation owners in that it does not have to pay federal income tax on any profits attributable to it (state rules vary). This can make an ESOP very attractive in some cases. It also makes converting to S corporation status very appealing when a C corporation's ESOP owns a high percentage of the company's stock.

For S corporation owners who want to use an ESOP to provide a market for their shares, generally it will make sense to convert to C status before setting up an ESOP. Where selling shares is not a priority, or where the seller either does not have substantial capital gains taxes due on the sale or has other reasons to retain S corporation status, an S corporation ESOP can provide significant tax benefits. However, keep in mind that any distributions paid to owners must be paid pro-rata to the ESOP. The ESOP can use these distributions to purchase additional shares, to build up cash for future repurchases of employee shares, or just to add to employee accounts.

While the S corporation rules make an ESOP very attractive, legislation passed in 2001 makes it clear that companies may not create an ESOP primarily to benefit a few people. For instance, some accountants were promoting plans in which a company would set up an S corporation management company owned by just a few people that would manage a large C corporation. The C corporation's profits would flow through the S corporation's ESOP and thus not be taxed.

The rules Congress enacted are complicated, but they boil down to two essential points. First, people who own more than 10% of the "deemed-owned" shares, or who own 20% counting their family members, are considered "disqualified" persons. "Deemed-owned shares" is defined to include what is allocated in the ESOP, a pro-rata share of unallocated shares in the trust, and any synthetic equity rights, such as phantom stock, stock options, stock appreciation rights, warrants, and certain kinds of deferred compensation the IRS considers equity-rights equivalents. Second, if these disqualified people together own 50% or more of the company's equity (counting their synthetic equity), then there will be devastating tax penalties. Congress also directed the IRS to apply this onerous tax treatment to any plan it deems to be substantially for the purpose of evading taxes rather than providing employee benefits.

Financial Issues for Employees

When an employee receives a distribution from the plan, it is taxable unless rolled over into an IRA or other qualified account. Otherwise, the amounts contributed by the employer are taxable as ordinary income, while any appreciation on the shares is taxable as capital gains. In addition, if the employee receives the distribution before normal retirement age and does not roll over the funds, a 10% excise tax is added.

While the stock is in the plan, however, it is not taxable to employees. It is rare, moreover, for employees to give up wages to participate in an ESOP or to purchase stock directly through a plan (this raises difficult securities law issues for closely held firms). Most ESOPs either are in addition to existing benefit plans or replace other defined contribution plans, usually at a higher contribution level.

Accounting

In nonleveraged plans, the contribution to the ESOP shows up directly as a compensation cost. In leveraged plans, the principal payments and dividend payments on unallocated shares that are used to repay a loan show up as a compensation charge as well; dividends on allocated shares show up as a charge to retained earnings. The debt of the ESOP shows up as corporate debt, with an offsetting contra equity account that is reduced as the loan is repaid.

Ownership, Corporate Culture, and Corporate Performance

Many executives believe that if they share ownership and explain it well enough to people, then employees will perform better. It is not that simple, however. Employee ownership can improve corporate performance significantly, but only when combined with what we call an "ownership culture." Ownership culture companies share financial information with employees on a regular basis and get employees involved in work-level decisions. They seek out not just more employee effort to do the same things better, but more employee ideas to do things better—or do new things entirely.

On the financial level, these companies typically share some version of the income statement and balance sheet on a periodic basis. More important, they break numbers down into usable small pieces that measure key performance issues for the company and for employee groups, such as quality control, output, backlog, customer satisfaction, on-time delivery, etc. These numbers provide employees with targets they can easily grasp and work to meet or exceed. The best companies get employees involved in generating these numbers as well.

Employees also have regular opportunities for input through work teams, quality circles, ad hoc committees, suggestion systems, informal and formal meetings with managers, and other opportunities. Management does not just pay lip service to the idea of empowering employees to make more decisions; it really does it. Ownership culture companies find that, over time, employee ideas get better and better, and that more of the work force becomes engaged in finding ways to help the company make money.

Conclusion

ESOPs are hard work. They take time to understand and implement; it takes even more time and effort to create a true ownership culture.

But go to an ESOP meeting and you will meet company leaders who are not just glad they did it, but absolutely evangelical. Not only are they succeeding and enjoying the tax benefits of ESOPs, but they are also just flat-out having more fun. ESOPs are not right for everyone, but if you are willing to make this effort, they are well worth considering.

CHAPTER 2

Selling to an ESOP in a Closely Held Company

Scott Rodrick

s chapter 1 states, the most popular use of an ESOP is to buy the shares of a departing owner in a closely held company. This chapter goes into more detail on why this happens and discusses the rules for a major tax incentive for selling owners in C corporations, the tax-deferred "rollover" of funds from an ESOP sale, plus some major considerations that go into deciding whether to sell to an ESOP and whether to elect the tax-deferred "rollover."

Why a Sale to an ESOP Often Makes Sense

An ESOP is not for everyone, but in many cases, it is the best way for someone to sell shares in a closely held company they own. As a tax-exempt employee benefit plan trust, the ESOP offers flexible, tax-advantaged treatment and does not have the restrictions, covenants, employment consequences, and other problems that can arise with an outside buyer.

The ESOP Creates a Market for the Shares in Any Amount

After years of building their companies, many small business owners find themselves at an impasse when the time comes to leave. Sometimes a family member or members may be willing and able to take over, but even then, the owner may wish to sell part or all of his or her ownership interest, and it may not be practical for personal or financial reasons for family members to buy out the owner. Company managers or other employees may be interested in buying shares, but buying the entire company may be financially unfeasible. Moving beyond the sphere of family members and employees, the owner may seek an outside buyer, but that too can be difficult (and expensive if a business broker is used).

If the would-be seller owns a minority interest in the company, or owns more but wants to sell only a part of the company, outside buyers may not be interested. Often, there are multiple owners of a closely held company, and at any given time, only a few may be interested in selling. And even if several people want to sell, their interests may still amount to a small percentage. The remaining owners may not want to deal with the proposed new owners.

An ESOP solves these dilemmas by creating a market for the shares. It can buy any percentage of the company; thus, an owner or owners can sell anything from a small percentage to all of the company to the ESOP.

Owners Can Sell Gradually to the ESOP While Staying with the Business

A potential buyer, especially an outside one, often will want to buy an owner's interest all at once. In contrast, an ESOP is flexible and, in addition to being able to buy any percentage of the shares (as noted above), can buy shares gradually so the owner can slowly exit his or her investment.

If the selling owner is the CEO or holds another major executive position at the company, an outside buyer often will wish to replace him or her with someone else (perhaps retaining the owner as a consultant for some period). If the ESOP is the buyer, however, there is no need for the selling owner to leave the company unless he or she desires to.

An ESOP Preserves the Stability of the Company

Sometimes people worry that since rank-and-file employees become beneficial owners through the ESOP trust, the company will be turned upside down and "the inmates will run the asylum." The truth is actually the opposite. If someone sells a company to an outsider, especially one that merely wants the company for its assets or to gain a strategic advantage over a competitor, the seller may wake up one day to find that all the managers have been fired (they are often the first people to be discarded or replaced), that beloved rank-and-file employees have been fired, or even that the company has been shut down after being stripped of its assets. With an ESOP, in contrast, the company stays the same; the only difference is that the stock now happens to be held by an employee trust (the ESOP trust) instead of the former owners. The ESOP trustee, selected by the company's board, in turn votes for the board in the trustee's capacity as a shareholder, unless the company chooses to pass the vote through to the ESOP participants.[1]

Employees Will Gain Ownership and Motivation

From the seller's point of view, an ESOP provides an excellent market for company shares. Something else to consider is that employees will gain a valuable benefit (i.e., stock in their ESOP accounts). Furthermore, as discussed elsewhere in this book, the combination of employee ownership through an ESOP and a management style that recognizes that ownership can result in a more motivated workforce and thus a more profitable company.

---

1. In that case, the trustee would still vote the shares (because the ESOP trust is the shareholder), but would do so as instructed by the ESOP participants. The company would do this by having the ESOP plan document drafted to provide for such voting rights.

An ESOP Is Cost-Effective for the Owner and Company

If a business broker is used to sell the company to an outside buyer, a large fee may be charged. Aside from this, the selling owner will have to pay what may be an enormous tax bill if it is a cash transaction. It is possible to structure a company sale as a tax-free reorganization in which another company acquires the seller's company in exchange for stock. Again, this raises the issue of having to sell most or all of the company, which may not be desirable or even possible, given other owners or a desire to sell only a part of the company. And, depending on the transaction structure, the company may cease to exist, at least in its old form. Finally, the owner ends up with an undiversified investment in somebody else's company and has two choices: either keep that stock and pray that it does not lose value as the years go by and that it can be sold someday, or sell the stock now and pay taxes.

Alternatively, the owner may seek a sale by corporate redemption, but this is not tax-efficient for anyone because the owner pays taxes and the company receives no tax deduction.

In contrast, an ESOP offers considerable tax advantages. The company's contributions to pay for the buyout are tax-deductible. This means, for example, that a $3 million sale to the ESOP does not require the company to first earn $5 million or so, pay taxes, and then take the $3 million remaining to fund the buyout. With an ESOP, the funds used to buy out an owner ($3 million in this example) are pretax.

In a C corporation, the owner can indefinitely defer taxation on the proceeds of the transaction by reinvesting them in securities of U.S. companies and electing the Section 1042 tax deferral (discussed below). In an S corporation, the Section 1042 tax deferral is not available. However, there is a separate tax advantage: there will be no federal tax (and, depending on the state, often no state tax) on corporate income attributable to the ESOP, which means that the company will not need to pay distributions to fund tax bills if the ESOP owns all of the company.

The Section 1042 Tax-Deferred Rollover

For countless business owners over the years, one of the main reasons for selling to an ESOP has been the ability to indefinitely postpone taxation on the gains by electing tax-deferred "rollover" treatment under Section 1042 of the Internal Revenue Code (the "Code"). In a nutshell, when an owner in a closely held C corporation sells to an ESOP that owns 30% or more of the company (including the amount the ESOP holds after the transaction), the seller can defer taxation indefinitely by "rolling over" the sales proceeds into stocks and bonds of U.S. companies (the "Section 1042 rollover," also referred to here by such terms as "the Section 1042 tax deferral" or "Section 1042 treatment"). Furthermore, if the selling owner holds the newly bought stocks or bonds until death, there will be a step-up in basis, and his or her heirs will pay no capital gains tax. Section 1042 treatment does not arise automatically; the selling owner must formally elect the tax deferral and file required paperwork, as described below.

Currently, Section 1042 is not as important as it once was in the ESOP community. Capital gains rates were quite low for some years and even as of 2014 are not as high as they once were. However, the Section 1042 rollover remains an important consideration, and it is the only ESOP tax incentive that is given to the selling owner.

There are many requirements for the tax deferral, so they will be discussed one by one.

The Company Must Be a Closely Held C Corporation

Section 1042 applies only to a sale to an ESOP in a C corporation. An S corporation can allow selling owners to elect the Section 1042 tax deferral by converting to C status before the ESOP transaction. If it does this, however, it must wait at least five years before re-electing S status.

The company must be closely held as well: for at least one year before and after the sale, the company (and each corporation belonging to a controlled group of corporations with the company) must have no stock that is tradable on "an established securities market."

The ESOP Must Own 30% or More of the Company After the Sale

The ESOP need not hold any shares before the sale, and the sale itself need not be of any particular amount, but after the sale, the ESOP must own 30% or more of either each class of outstanding stock or the total value of all of the company's outstanding stock (excluding in each case nonvoting, nonconvertible preferred stock).[2]

Two or more sellers may aggregate their sales to meet the "30% after the sale" requirement if the sales are part of a single, integrated transaction that they prearrange. For example, if owner X and owner Y each sell 15% of the company in such an integrated transaction, the IRS will not say, "The ESOP held only 15% after owner X sold, so X cannot elect Section 1042 treatment"; rather, it will look at the entire transaction, in which the ESOP ended up with 30%.

In determining what constitutes 30% ownership, Section 1042(b) (2) applies Code Section 318(a)(4), which provides that "[i]f any person has an option to acquire stock, such stock shall be considered as owned by such person." For example, if the ESOP would otherwise own 30% of the company after the transaction but someone has an option (or equivalent security such as a warrant) to buy shares in

---

2. Thus, an ESOP could be formed, holding no stock at first, and then a 30% sale made, which would allow the selling owner to elect the tax deferral on all of the sale proceeds. Alternatively, an ESOP could have been established some years ago and hold 29% of the company. The owner could now sell 1%, upon which the 30% threshold would have been reached, allowing the Section 1042 tax deferral to take place. However, the owner could elect Section 1042 treatment only on that 1% because, as explained below, the tax-deferred reinvestment in other securities must take place between 3 months before the sale and 12 months after, and the other 29% was sold years ago in this example.

an amount that would dilute the ESOP's ownership under 30%, the transaction will fail the 30% test.

The Seller Must Be an Individual or One of Certain Other Entities

To elect the Section 1042 tax deferral, a seller must be an individual, a partnership, a (taxable) trust, an estate, or a limited liability company (LLC). The seller cannot be a C nor (apparently) an S corporation. If the seller is a partnership or LLC, the partnership or LLC makes the 1042 election, not individual partners or members.

The Stock Must Have Been Held for Three Years and Cannot Be from a Qualified Stock Plan

Generally speaking, the selling owner must have held the stock for three years before the sale. However, if the seller had an asset or business interest that was exchanged in a tax-free transaction for stock in the company that now is setting up the ESOP (for example, if the company was recently formed through the exchange of stock for an existing asset), the holding period of the asset will be "tacked" to the holding period of the stock, and the three-year rule will be met. Additionally, if the selling owner acquired the stock as a gift, the donor's holding period can likewise be "tacked" on to the owner's holding period to meet the three-year rule.

The stock cannot have been acquired through a distribution from a tax-qualified retirement plan or through an option or company stock purchase arrangement. For example, this means that ESOP participants who receive stock cannot elect the Section 1042 tax deferral if they sell the stock back to the company.

The Seller Must Reinvest the Gains in Stocks or Bonds of U.S. Companies

To elect the Section 1042 tax deferral, the seller must reinvest in "qualified replacement property" (QRP) during the period beginning

3 months before and ending 12 months after the sale date. QRP must consist of stocks, bonds, or other such equity instruments such as debentures. It must be issued by domestic (i.e., U.S.-based) operating corporations that obtain no more than 25% of their gross income from passive investments (such as income from royalties, rents, etc.).[3] QRP does not include mutual funds, U.S. or municipal bonds, or real estate investment trusts (REITs). Securities of the company sponsoring the ESOP are ineligible, but QRP can include stock of other companies owned by the seller as long as they are not in the same controlled group of corporations as the ESOP sponsor. There are long-term floating-rate corporate securities, often called "ESOP Notes," that are specifically designed to serve as QRP.

The QRP needs to qualify as such only when the seller buys it. If the seller buys and records securities as QRP but they later stop qualifying (e.g., if the seller buys stock of a U.S. company that later reincorporates outside the U.S.), the QRP will not be disqualified.

The funds used to buy the QRP need not literally come from the ESOP transaction, so the "reinvestment" is not necessarily a rollover of proceeds from the sale, although it very often is. However, the tax that is deferred is the tax that would be paid on proceeds from the ESOP sale, so the maximum amount that can be invested in QRP is the amount coming from the ESOP sale. Note that the seller need not elect the Section 1042 tax deferral for all of the proceeds; for example, he or she can reinvest 50% of the proceeds in QRP and pay tax on the other 50%.

The Seller Must Meet Section 1042's Procedural Requirements

To qualify for the Section 1042 tax deferral, the seller must make three kinds of filings:

---

3. There is an exception to the passive investment rule for certain financial institutions and for insurance companies subject to taxation.

1. *Statement of election.* The seller must formally elect Section 1042 treatment in a "statement of election" attached to the seller's tax return for the taxable year in which the sale to the ESOP occurs.

2. *Statement of purchase.* For every purchase of QRP (remember, all such purchases must take place within the single 15-month window described above), the seller must execute and have notarized a "statement of purchase." This formerly had to be notarized within 30 days after the purchase, but the IRS currently allows it to be notarized not later than the filing of the seller's tax return for the year in which the election was made, or, if the QRP was purchased later, not later than the filing of the seller's tax return for the next year. Every statement of purchase is filed with the seller's tax return.

3. *Statement of consent from the company.* The seller must file with the statement of election a verified written statement from the company (i.e., the employer sponsoring the ESOP) consenting to the application of the excise tax provisions under Code Section 4978 (a 10% tax if the ESOP disposes of the shares from the Section 1042 transaction within three years) and Code Section 2979A (a 50% tax if a prohibited allocation is made under the ESOP).

The Seller Will Pay Tax If Any QRP Is Sold

The QRP holdings are *not* like an IRA or other tax-deferred account within which people may buy and sell without paying tax. Instead, the seller will pay tax if he or she sells or otherwise disposes of any QRP (but only on the QRP that was disposed of).[4] Thus, within 12 months after the ESOP sale, the seller must make investment decisions that he or she will live with until death if tax is to continue to

---

4. For purposes of computing the tax, the basis of the QRP is the basis of the stock sold to the ESOP. There is no tax if the QRP is disposed if in certain transactions, such as a donation of QRP to a charity.

be deferred. If the QRP is held until the seller dies, there will be a step-up in basis, and the seller's heirs will pay no tax.

If the QRP is a bond and it reaches its stated maturity date, or the QRP is a callable bond (i.e., the issuer can redeem it before it matures) and it is called, that counts as a disposition, and the seller will pay tax.

To get around the pay-tax-if-you-sell limitation of QRP, some sellers buy long-term, noncallable bonds and hold them to avoid paying taxes but borrow against them and invest freely in the market.

The Company Must Hold the Shares for at Least Three Years to Avoid an Excise Tax

As noted above in the discussion of procedural requirements, the company generally will pay an excise tax if, within three years after a transaction in which the seller elected Section 1042 treatment, the ESOP disposes of securities acquired in the transaction. However, the actual rule does not literally trace the shares sold to the ESOP in the Section 1042 transaction. Rather, the excise tax is imposed if, during that three-year period after the sale, (1) the total number of shares in the ESOP is less than the number of shares it held immediately after the ESOP transaction or (2) the value of stock in the ESOP is less than 30% of the value of all company securities as of the date of the disposition.

The rule does not apply to tax-free stock exchanges; dispositions to meet the ESOP diversification requirements; or benefit distributions made by reason of death, retirement after age 59½, disability, or a separation from service resulting in a one-year break in service.

The ESOP Is Prohibited from Allocating Shares from the Sale to the Seller, the Seller's Relatives, and More-Than-25% Shareholders

Under the prohibited allocation rule governing Section 1042 sales, when a selling shareholder elects the Section 1042 tax deferral, the

ESOP is forbidden from allocating stock from that transaction to the seller, certain relatives of the seller, and more-than-25% stockholders.

For the later of (1) 10 years after the sale or (2) the date of the final allocation of stock from the sale if it was a leveraged transaction, the ESOP cannot allocate shares from the Section 1042 transaction to either selling shareholders who have elected Section 1042 treatment or to certain close relatives (siblings, spouses, ancestors, and lineal descendants).[5]

So long as shares from the Section 1042 transaction remain in the ESOP, they cannot be allocated to more-than-25% shareholders, defined as owners of more than 25% of any class of stock, more than 25% of the value of any class of stock, or more than 25% of any class of stock (or the value thereof) in a member of the same controlled group of corporations. Shares owned by certain parties such as parents, spouses, children, and grandchildren are attributed to the person, as are any ESOP-held shares allocated to the person's ESOP account, plus shares represented by stock options or similar instruments (warrants or convertible debentures). In testing for more than 25% ownership, the one-year period ending with the sale date and the date the stock from the sale is allocated are counted.

There is one exception to the prohibited allocation rule: a total of 5% of the stock from the Section 1042 transaction can be allocated to the ESOP accounts of the seller's lineal descendants. However, in many cases, the lineal descendants are more-than-25% owners by attribution and thus are excluded from the ESOP.

The company cannot use a tax-qualified retirement plan to reward employees who are prevented from receiving ESOP allocations under this rule; however, it can use equity incentives such as stock options.[6]

---

5. The IRS has ruled that if multiple sellers elect Section 1042 treatment, they are mutually excluded from allocations attributable to each other's shares.

6. Also note that the prohibited allocation rule applies only to shares from transactions in which the seller elected Section 1042 treatment. The ESOP may hold other shares that may be allocated to the seller, his or her relatives, and more-than-25% shareholders. However, the ESOP cannot make up the

If the prohibited allocation rule is violated, the person in question is taxed as though he or she has received a taxable distribution of the allocation, and the company sponsoring the ESOP pays a 50% excise tax on the amount of the allocation.

Planning Considerations

Choosing Whether to Elect Section 1042 Treatment

The Section 1042 tax deferral has been a major advantage for many sellers over the years, but sometimes it is not worth using, as in the following situations:

When the company is an S corporation and Section 1042 would offer little benefit. As noted above, one requirement for the Section 1042 tax deferral is that the company must be a C corporation, so an S corporation could revoke its S status and become a C corporation so the owner could elect Section 1042 treatment. One problem with this is that the company would then have to wait five years to re-elect S status, which would be undesirable in some situations. Also, Section 1042 holds little value for some S shareholders. In S corporations where distributions are relatively minimal, shareholders can accumulate a relatively high basis in their shares, meaning that there is little taxation when they sell their interest in the company. In such cases, Section 1042 is often more trouble than it is worth, especially since the company will not have the tax advantages of S status while it is a C corporation.

When too many crucial people would be excluded from the ESOP. As noted above, certain family members of the seller (except for a narrow exception), plus more-than-25% shareholders, are excluded from receiving ESOP allocations attributable to the transaction. In

---

difference between these persons and other ESOP participants by contributing extra cash or other non-employer-stock assets to their accounts.

some cases, this is unacceptable, and the seller thus goes forward with an ESOP transaction but does elect Section 1042 treatment.

When the seller wishes to pay tax now and invest freely without regard to the limitations of QRP and potential future taxes. The ESOP rules are very limiting for some sellers who reinvest under Section 1042 because they are limited in their investment choices (no mutual funds, for example) and because the tax deferral will end if and when they ever sell their QRP. For some people, this is a good reason to pay tax now, take the post-tax proceeds, and invest freely. Additionally, some sellers believe that future capital gains tax rates will be higher, in which case they would pay more in taxes if they acquired QRP and then sold it later on instead of paying tax now.

Seller Financing and Section 1042

As the chapter on financing in this book notes, seller financing (in which the selling owner receives a note from the ESOP for some or all of the sale price) is becoming increasingly popular. This creates issues when the seller wishes to elect Section 1042, however. Seller financing means that the seller will receive a stream of payments from the ESOP over a period of years, but the Section 1042 tax deferral is available only to the extent that the seller purchases QRP within 12 months after the transaction. If the seller does not have other funds available to invest in QRP within 12 months after the sale (as noted above, QRP need not be bought with the actual proceeds of the sale to the ESOP), then he or she cannot fully take advantage of Section 1042. This potentially means that electing Section 1042 treatment would have no value for an owner involved in a self-financed sale to an ESOP. However, the seller can borrow the money to buy QRP and then use income from the QRP to repay the loan taken out to buy it. This is usually done by buying "ESOP Notes," non-callable bonds qualifying as QRP. Banks will usually loan up to 90% of the face value of such bonds.

The Section 1042 Deferral in Mergers and Acquisitions

There is a trend in the ESOP community to use the ESOP as a vehicle for acquisitions. When an ESOP company seeks to acquire another company, the parties may desire to allow the owner of the target corporation to take advantage of Section 1042—an opportunity that would give the acquiring company a competitive edge in the acquisitions market.

The problem is that the ESOP is in the acquiring company, whereas the target owner's stock is in the target company. There are a few ways to deal with this. For example, the acquiring company can be merged into the target company in a reverse merger, followed by a sale to an ESOP by the target's owner in which he or she elects Section 1042 treatment. Or both companies, not just the acquirer, could set up ESOPs (in which the target's owner would elect Section 1042 treatment), followed by a merger. In yet another approach, the target company merges into the acquirer in exchange for shares in the acquirer, whereupon the target's owner sells the newly acquired shares of the acquirer to its ESOP and elects Section 1042 treatment. In any case, to qualify for Section 1042 treatment, the target's owner must have owned the shares for at least three years (or otherwise meet the three-year holding requirement described above) before the sale to the ESOP.

Valuation Considerations

As the chapter on valuation in this book explains, all ESOP transactions involving company stock in a closely held company must be based on a valuation from an independent appraiser. Moreover, the ESOP cannot pay more than fair market value for the shares it acquires. The appraised price for ESOP purposes may reflect a discount for lack of control if a non-controlling interest would be sold to the plan (a majority or other interest giving the owner voting control over the company is worth more than a non-controlling interest). The appraised price may reflect a further discount for lack of marketability (i.e., since the company is closely held).

For some sellers, this may become an issue if another potential buyer (perhaps a competing business willing to pay a premium for the company) offers more money than the ESOP would pay. In such a situation, the seller must weigh the tax and other advantages of an ESOP against the higher price being offered. In some situations, the ESOP buys part of the company and the outside buyer buys the rest. (This in turn raises the issue of whether the ESOP and the outside buyer will get the same shares for the same price; see the valuation chapter for details.)

Charitable Contributions and ESOPs

Many owners who sell to an ESOP have charitable intentions for at least some of their sales proceeds. Such sellers may find it advantageous to use a charitable remainder trust (CRT), a tax-exempt, irrevocable trust designed to pay out its assets to a charity. With a CRT, the seller makes a contribution of securities to the trust and in return receives a tax deduction for the contribution (in the amount of its actuarially calculated remainder interest), plus an income stream for a specified period or for life. This can provide the owner with more income than a simple donation outside the ESOP context in which the owner first sells the stock, pays taxes, and then contributes the remaining money to the charity.

One way to use a CRT is for a C corporation owner to sell to an ESOP, elect Section 1042 treatment, reinvest some or all of the proceeds in QRP, and contribute some or all of the QRP to the CRT; this contribution constitutes a tax-free disposition of the QRP. The seller then receives a tax deduction, plus a stream of income from the CRT. The charity receives a larger contribution than it would have otherwise because the Section 1042 tax deferral allows the seller to contribute all the money from the sale instead of paying taxes and then contributing the remainder.

Another way to use a CRT is for the selling owner not to sell to the ESOP at all, at least not for the amount that the CRT is to receive. Rather, the seller contributes his or her company stock directly to the CRT, which sells it to the ESOP. (This is facilitated by a prearranged understanding among the parties that this sale will occur.) Again, the seller receives a tax deduction and income stream.

Alternatively, the seller may dispense with a CRT and instead simply contribute QRP to a charity, providing both a larger contribution for the charity and a larger tax deduction for the seller. However, there will be no income stream for the seller.

The main downside of any of these approaches is that the selling owner no longer has the securities that have been contributed and thus cannot leave those securities to his or her heirs. In any case, a charitable donation works best for business owners with a serious charitable intent.

CHAPTER 3

ESOPs in S Corporations

Corey Rosen

T he most-tax favored business form in the U.S. today is an ESOP-owned S corporation. Until 1998, ESOPs and other non-taxable entities could not own shares in an S corporation, but that law was changed so that starting in 1998, non-taxed entities could own S stock, provided they paid tax on the earnings at the highest personal rate. Congress specifically decided, however, that ESOPs, and only ESOPs, should not have to pay any tax. So if the ESOP owned 30% of the stock, tax would not have to be paid on 30% of the profits of the company; if it owned 100%, no tax would be due. This is not a loophole in the law but a considered and discussed congressional choice to encourage employee ownership.

As a result of this, there has been an explosion of S corporation ESOPs. While many of these are in S corporations that set up an ESOP to buy a minority ownership stake, the majority are 100% ESOP-owned companies, usually conversions from C corporations with ESOPs. While a few of these C ESOPs were already 100% ESOP-owned, most were companies that saw the opportunity to acquire this highly favored tax status, had the ESOP buy the remaining shares, and elected S status. We estimate that perhaps 40% or more of all ESOPs are in S corporations, and 20% or so of all ESOP companies are now 100% ESOP-owned. Because this topic is so important, we have placed this chapter early in the book.

Although S corporation ESOPs have unique tax advantages, they also have some limitations compared to C ESOPs. The basic attributes of S corporation ESOPs are summarized below:

1. Profits attributable to ESOP ownership of S corporation stock are exempt from federal income tax. Thus, a 100% ESOP-owned S corporation becomes the only form of corporate structure Congress intentionally exempted from federal income tax.

2. Sellers to ESOPs in S corporation ESOPs cannot qualify for the Section 1042 deferral of capital gains taxes available to qualifying sellers to ESOPs in C corporations.

3. Interest paid on ESOP loans in S corporation ESOPs counts toward the maximum amount that can be contributed to the plan, whereas it generally does not in C corporation ESOPs.

4. S corporations cannot deduct dividends (or "distributions," as they are called in S corporations) that are used to repay an ESOP loan, that are passed through to participants, or that participants reinvest in company stock. S corporation distributions can be used to repay the loan, however.

5. S corporation ESOPs designed primarily to benefit one person or a small number of people, including those intended solely or principally to benefit management or existing corporate owners, will potentially be subject to severe tax penalties.

S Corporations and ESOPs: The Evolution of the Law

The S corporation is a form of business ownership in which the corporation does not pay tax on its earnings. Instead, owners of the S corporation pay tax on their proportionate share of the company's earnings at their own individual tax rates. S corporations often pay a distribution to these owners roughly equal to the amount of tax they owe. When owners of an S corporation sell their ownership interest, they pay capital gains taxes on the gain. Their basis is increased by allocations of earnings on which they have paid taxes. S corporations allow owners to avoid the double taxation on corporate earnings that must be paid in C corporations (the company pays taxes on profits; the owners pay taxes when the profits are distributed). S corporations can have only one class of stock and no more than 100 owners.

Until 1998, S corporations could not have an ESOP that owned stock in the company, because ESOPs are non-profit trusts, which could not own stock in an S corporation because the trust would not pay tax, thus allowing a portion of the earnings to go untaxed. In 1997, Congress exempted S corporation ESOPs (and, among trusts that can be S corporation owners, only ESOPs) from the unrelated business income tax (UBIT). Effectively, ESOP participants pay this tax when their shares are distributed to them (their basis in the shares would be lower than that of other owners who had paid tax, so their taxable gain would be higher), but participants have the option of rolling their distributions into an IRA and deferring tax further. The law also allows S corporations to require that departing employees take their distributions in the form of cash rather than stock, thus avoiding the potential disqualification that could occur if an employee put the stock into an IRA (IRAs and other non-ESOP retirement trusts cannot own S corporation shares).

Although these changes made ESOPs both possible and attractive in S corporations, S corporation ESOPs do not have all the same tax benefits that a C corporation ESOP has. Under Internal Revenue Code Section 1042, owners selling to an ESOP in a closely held C corporation can defer taxation on any gain they report from the sale of stock to an ESOP owning 30% or more of the company's shares; S corporation owners cannot. C corporations sponsoring ESOPs can deduct up to 25% of the eligible pay of ESOP participants to repay the principal on an ESOP loan, and interest payments on the loan do not count toward these limits. They can deduct up to 25% of eligible pay for additional contributions to the ESOP or other retirement plans not used to repay the loan as well; S corporations are limited to 25% for all defined contribution plans. Eligible pay excludes pay over $250,000 per year (in 2012; this number is adjusted upward annually), pay of employees not in the plan, and any other pay the plan document defines as ineligible. In S corporations, however, interest payments are included in the 25% limit, thus lowering the amount that can be contributed.

In both S and non-leveraged C corporations, corporate contributions to an ESOP are added to corporate contributions to other retirement plans to test for compliance with the 25%-of-eligible-pay limit on corporate contributions, but leveraged ESOPs can treat the plans separately. Also, no one can have more than $50,000 in contributions to retirement plans (as of 2012), including company and employee contributions, added to their account in any one year. The combination of contributions also cannot exceed 100% of any individual's annual pay.

C corporation ESOPs also can deduct dividends used to repay an ESOP loan, dividends that are passed directly through to participants, or dividends participants voluntarily reinvest in company stock in the ESOP. S corporations technically do not pay dividends. Instead, they make distributions of earnings to shareholders. While these may be functionally comparable to dividends in C corporations, they are not technically the same and are not considered dividends for the purposes of tax deductions. S corporations that are 100% owned by an ESOP, of course, do not need to be concerned about deductibility. They don't pay federal income tax anyway. But for less-than-100% ESOPs in S corporations, the non-deductibility of dividends could increase taxes for other shareholders.

Issues in Deciding on Whether to Use an S or C Structure

For S corporation owners considering setting up an ESOP, the ability to avoid taxation on the ESOP's share of earnings is a powerful tax incentive. Where the goal of the ESOP is simply to provide a benefit to employees, or the sellers believe it makes more sense to go ahead and pay capital gains taxes now, there may be no reason to convert to C status. There are other possible considerations, however, in deciding to stay S.

Where the ESOP Is Being Used to Buy Out an Owner

Normally, if an owner wants to sell, an S corporation will first convert to C status so the seller can defer gain on the sale. There are several scenarios, however, where owners of an S corporation may not want to do this:

1. *The seller is not the only owner.* While the seller benefits from the conversion to C status, the other owners now find any of their earnings that would have been sheltered from the corporate-level tax no longer are. If the sale does not create enough deductions to reduce the corporate-level tax low enough to satisfy these owners, they may not want to convert. Note, however, that the other owners may not face this problem if the C corporation ESOP creates enough debt or contribution obligations to reduce or eliminate the corporate-level tax. Also, earnings that would have been paid out to the owner in a S corporation could be paid out as compensation to those owners in a C corporation, creating almost as advantageous a tax situation because the corporation could deduct the compensation (note, however, that the compensation cannot be unreasonable, as defined by the IRS, and that it will, unlike distributed earnings in the S corporation, be subject to payroll tax).

2. *There are large amounts of undistributed earnings.* When the conversion to C status takes place, any earnings that have not yet been contributed to the owners must be distributed in one year or they are taxable to the owners (meaning they will be taxed twice, since the owners have already paid tax on them before). If the company does not have the cash to do this, it could borrow

money, but the ESOP may itself require too much cash to make this payout practical.

3. *Sellers plan to sell the company in an asset sale.* In an S corporation, the sale of the company's assets trigger only a single tax at the individual level; in a C corporation, the sale would be taxed at both the corporate and individual level, as income to the company and as capital gains to the individuals. The amount of the corporate tax would depend in part on the depreciation taken on the assets.

4. *The S corporation is creating losses the owners want flowed through to them.* In some situations, a company may be making heavy investments, often in real property or other hard assets, that create paper losses. These losses can be flowed through to the owners, who can deduct them at a marginally higher rate than can the company. In some scenarios, this may be desirable.

5. *The seller's basis is already very high because of taxes paid on previously undistributed earnings.* In this case, the "rollover" provision may not make much difference.

6. *There are multiple classes of stock, and it is important for the company or the ESOP to retain this feature.* For instance, if the ESOP has convertible preferred shares, changing to an S corporation would require they be converted to common shares. In some cases, this may not be practical. There is also a fiduciary issue for the conversion (whether it is in the interest of the ESOP participants as shareholders to convert) that could affect this transaction.

7. *The seller, the seller's family members, or other 25% owners are employees.* If the seller chooses to defer taxes on gains on the sale to a C corporation ESOP, neither the seller, the seller's close family members, nor 25% owners can get allocations of stock in the ESOP from those shares. But if the seller does not elect the deferral (as would be the case if the company retains S

status), these people all can participate. The allocations may be substantial and offset a large part of the potential tax deferral that is foregone.

Cash Flow Considerations in Less-Than-100% ESOPs

Where a company is 100% owned by an ESOP, conversion to an S is often a foregone conclusion. Why pay taxes when you don't have to? Barring special issues relating to converting from an S to a C, converting in 100% ownership situations is the norm. But where the ESOP owns less than 100% of the stock, the considerations are more complex.

Most S corporations make distributions to their shareholders in amounts at least large enough to cover their tax obligations. Because S corporations can have only one class of stock, if distributions are paid they must be paid to the ESOP as well. Because the ESOP does not pay taxes, the distributions it receives can create a pool of cash that can be used to buy additional shares or pay off a loan. Any leftover distributions could be used to fund repurchase obligations. The distributions could also be used to buy more stock in the company. This would dilute the existing owners' percentage of ownership but not their value (because an equivalent amount of cash had been brought back into the company). The company would now have additional cash.

Where the ESOP owns less than 100% of the stock, special attention must be paid to cash flow issues. Assume the ESOP owns 50%, for instance, and the company elects S corporation status. Also assume the company makes distributions to shareholders in amounts at least sufficient to cover their taxes. Assume earnings of $1 million and that the personal tax rate of the owners is 40%. The company thus pays a distribution of $200,000 to the non-ESOP owners and $200,000 to the ESOP. Total retained earnings are now $600,000. If the company remained a C corporation and paid 38% state and federal tax on the $1 million earnings, it would have $620,000 in retained earnings. The payout to owners, however, will increase their basis and thus reduce their long-term capital gains obligation. If owners in this scenario did not want to pay out earnings but instead preferred to retain them for corporate reinvestment or did not want the additional $200,000 going to the ESOP, converting would not make sense.

Issues for C Corporations with ESOPs Converting to S Status

Many C corporations with ESOPs are considering switching to S status. Especially where the ESOP owns a substantial part of the company's stock, this can provide a substantial tax benefit, even reducing taxes to zero where the ESOP owns 100% of the shares. Indeed, it is arguably a duty of ESOP fiduciaries to consider such a switch. Several issues must be kept in mind, however:

- The election requires the consent of all shareholders.

- An S corporation can only have 100 shareholders (the ESOP counts as one). S corporations can have only one class of stock, with the one exception that they can have voting and nonvoting common shares. Some C corporation ESOPs use convertible preferred or super-common stock for various reasons. These may or may not be sufficiently compelling issues to warrant remaining a C corporation.

- An S corporation that uses last in, first out (LIFO) accounting and had been a C corporation before electing S status must pay a LIFO recapture tax (the amount by which the FIFO [first in, first out] inventory exceeds the LIFO inventory). This could be substantial in some cases, especially in capital-intensive businesses. If a company uses LIFO accounting procedures, there is an immediate recapture over four years of any excess inventory (not assets) with LIFO over what would have been the case with FIFO.

- For a 10-year period after conversion, if the company sells any asset it held on the day of its S corporation election, it will have to pay "built-in gains" tax on that sale. This tax is in addition to taxes paid by shareholders.

- In S corporations, some fringe benefits paid to 2%-or-more owners are taxable.

- Net operating losses incurred as a C corporation are suspended while the company remains an S corporation. These losses may be applied against LIFO or built-in gains taxes, however.

- State laws vary, and some states may not track federal laws, so S corporation ESOPs still may have some tax obligation.

- If there could be an eventual desire or need to switch back to C status, remember that there is a fiduciary issue over whether the switch back to C would require the ESOP to get something back in return for what it has given up as an S corporation owner. The ESOP trustee will have to make a decision about whether the conversion, as proposed, would benefit the ESOP participants or whether its terms need to be modified.

If a decision to switch is made, conversion must occur within 2½ months of the end of the fiscal year. Plan participants are not required to vote on the conversion. This is not one of the required ESOP voting issues because conversion is a matter of individual S corporation owner *elections* rather than an actual vote. A company, however, can choose to have employees direct the trustee as to the voting of the shares.

Note also that the taxable year of an S corporation is the calendar year unless there is a valid business purpose to have a different fiscal year. Avoiding taxes is not a valid business purpose. One allowable exception is that if shareholders owning more than half the shares have a tax year other than the calendar year or are switching to the corporation's tax year. So if a C corporation wants to convert to S status and is more than 50% owned by an ESOP, the ESOP trustee could seek IRS approval for the S corporation to have other than a calendar-year tax year.

Operational Issues for S Corporation ESOPs

Valuation

S corporation ESOPs must pay particular attention to valuation issues. As with all ESOPs, all transactions involving the plan must be at an appraised fair market value. At this point, there is no regulatory guidance about how the special tax benefits the ESOP provides should affect the appraised value, but most practitioners agree that the tax benefits should not be counted. That's because those tax benefits are dependent on the company being an ESOP. Appraisals assume a hypothetical third-party buyer. If the buyer purchases the ESOP's shares, there would be no more ESOP tax benefits.

Distributions of Earnings

In most S corporations, distributions are made annually to owners in amounts at least sufficient to enable them to pay their taxes. Even though the ESOP does not have to pay taxes on its share of earnings, it must receive a pro-rata share of any distributions.

Distributions can also be used by the ESOP to repay debt. The 2004 tax law made it clear that distributions on both allocated and unallocated ESOP shares could be used for this purpose.

Where distributions are not used to repay a loan, the distributions on allocated shares will be treated as earnings on shares and will be allocated according to account balances. Distributions on unallocated shares can be allocated based on account balances or the company's normal allocation formula for contributions. Adding distributions based on account balances may raise issues for the distributional impact of ESOPs on newer employees because most of the benefit would accrue to employees who had larger account balances.

Some companies might want to pass distributions through directly to employees, but this generally is not advisable. These distributions will normally be subject to a 10% excise tax on "early distributions." The pass-through would also require the consent of each employee and would be subject to taxation.

Distributions of Account Balances to Departing Employees

In C corporation ESOPs, employees generally can demand distributions, and companies can choose to make distributions, in the form of company stock. Employees can roll over that stock into an IRA. However, because S corporation rules do not allow for there to be more than 100 shareholders at any one time or for an IRA to hold stock, S corporation ESOPs must follow specific procedures for making distributions. If an S corporation ESOP wants to distribute shares to employees when they leave (because the company wants to buy back the shares or for some other reason), but wants to give employees the opportunity to roll over the distribution into an IRA, a company can craft its plan so that employees can either get stock and sell it back or get cash and roll it over. If the employee only gets stock that is held very briefly—one day to allow the company to buy it back, for instance—the IRS has ruled that this does not really constitute ownership for the 100-owner test. It also does not create any potential problems with taxes for the employee who rolls the cash into an IRA. The IRS, in a private letter ruling, has confirmed the acceptability of this approach.

Alternatively, the company can just convert the shares into cash before distribution. S corporation ESOP rules specifically allow plan sponsors to eliminate the normal right employees have to demand a distribution in the form of shares.

Rules for Preventing S Corporation ESOP Abuses

Soon after the law was passed allowing ESOPs to be owners in S corporations and not to have to pay tax on their share of corporate earnings, there was a predictable (if disheartening) rush by some financial advisors to propose ESOPs for clients who really were not interested in sharing ownership broadly with employees. In some cases, this might be for professional firms with one or a few employees. In others, schemes were proposed in which managers would create an S corporation management company to manage a larger operating company. The management company would charge a management fee to the operating company equal to a large percentage of its profits. Because the management company would be structured as an S corporation owned by its ESOP, there would be no tax on these profits. In a more complex approach, the management company would include the employees of the operating company in its ESOP (this is allowable in companies that are part of the same control group). Managers in the S corporation would then pay themselves substantial deferred compensation that would escape tax because the S corporation would be 100% owned by the ESOP.

ESOP experts argued that all of these scams were already precluded under general authority granted the IRS to disallow tax shelters that have no valid business purpose other than to shield people from tax. If this test did not work, IRS regulations provide that "if the plan is so designed as to amount to a subterfuge for the distribution of profits to shareholders, it will not qualify as a plan for the exclusive benefit of employees even though other employees who are not shareholders are also included under the plan."

To provide more specific prohibitions, as well as to buttress the general language giving the IRS power to rule against these scams, Congress included a draconian set of tax penalties in the 2001 tax law.

In addition to the specific rules set forth below, the IRS developed regulations to define existing plans as subject to this legislation, regardless of when they were established, if their purpose is "in substance, an avoidance or evasion of the prohibited allocation rule."

The law is quite complex. The simplest way to describe it is to say that it provides extreme tax penalties for plans designed to funnel most of their benefits to a small group of people who own most of the company, either directly and/or through the plan or through "synthetic" equity. Synthetic equity includes stock options, phantom stock, stock appreciation rights, stock warrants, and most kinds of deferred compensation whose payment represents a claim on the assets of the corporation. It is intentionally a very broad definition. To find out whether a plan is subject to the law, two steps need to be taken:

1. First, you must determine whether there are any "disqualified persons," defined as anyone who as an individual owns 10% or more, or as part of a family owns 20% or more, of the "deemed-owned shares." Deemed-owned shares are (a) shares allocated to an individual in the ESOP, (b) the individual's pro-rata share of unallocated ESOP stock, and (c) any synthetic equity. Anyone in this group is considered "disqualified." Note that this means someone does not have be an ESOP participant to be in this group. Family members include spouses, lineal ascendants or descendants, siblings and their children, and the spouses of any of these family members. Being a disqualified person does not mean, however, that this person cannot be in the ESOP or receive synthetic equity. For that to be the case, the disqualified persons must also meet the test in step two.

2. Second, determine whether disqualified persons together own at least 50% of all shares in the company. In making this determination, ownership is defined to include:[1]

   a. shares held directly

   b. shares owned through synthetic equity

   c. allocated or a pro-rata portion of unallocated shares owned through the ESOP

If disqualified persons own at least 50% of the stock of the company (through the ESOP, deferred compensation [including synthetic

---

1. Disqualified persons are considered to own shares held by certain relatives plus a proportionate amount of shares held by certain corporations and other entities they control.

equity such as options and phantom stock], and direct ownership), there is a "nonallocation year," which means that penalties will be imposed for the excessive concentration of equity in the company among this limited group of people. These individuals may not receive an allocation from the ESOP during that year without a substantial tax penalty. This includes allocations of forfeited stock from departing unvested participants. It would also be impermissible to make up for the nonallocation by allocating more synthetic equity. If such an allocation does occur, it is taxed as a distribution to the recipient and a 50% corporate excise tax would apply to the fair market value of the stock allocated. If synthetic equity is owned, a 50% excise tax would also apply to its value as well. In the first year in which this rule applies, there is a 50% tax on the fair market value of "deemed-owned shares" even if no additional allocations are made to those individuals that year (in other words, the tax applies simply if disqualified persons own more than 50% of the company in the first year).

Conclusion

S corporation ESOP tax laws are not an accident or loophole. Congress intended this result because a large majority of its members believed that employee ownership is a valuable way to improve productivity and create a more equitable distribution of ownership. Companies that currently have ESOPs and are principally owned by their plan should almost invariably take a very serious look at electing S status. Existing S corporations without ESOPs may find setting up a plan desirable as well, especially if their owners do not want to take advantage of the tax-deferred sale to an ESOP available through to owners of C corporations. For those who want to use an S corporation ESOP primarily to benefit a small number of people, while minimizing or bypassing altogether the law's intent to spread ownership broadly, the best advice is not to proceed. The rewards may seem great, but the risks are even greater.

CHAPTER 4

Things to Do with an ESOP Besides Buying Out the Owner

Corey Rosen

The most typical use of an ESOP is to provide a market for the shares of owners who want to sell all or part of their ownership interests. ESOPs are by no means limited to this application, however. They also can be used simply as an employee benefit plan, as a match to a 401(k) plan, to acquire new capital or other companies, to buy out a division of a company, to support the market for a thinly traded company's stock, or even, in a few select situations, to save a company that would otherwise close. This chapter looks at these other uses.

The ESOP as an Employee Benefit Plan

In many ESOP companies, the plan's purpose is simply to provide an incentive for employees linked to the company's performance. This kind of ESOP is conceptually and practically straightforward. The company typically will issue additional shares to contribute to the plan. These new shares dilute the interests of existing shareholders but also generate a tax deduction for the company equal to the fair market value of the stock contributed. Shares contributed to the plan are allocated to accounts for employees in the plan as they are contributed. Like other ESOP shares, they must be repurchased after employees terminate or retire.

In setting up a plan like this, companies must consider several issues. First, the issue of dilution must be faced. The simplest way to deal with this is to set an acceptable ceiling on dilution. For instance, assume the owners agree that they can accept a 25% dilution. When this figure is approached, the company can limit future stock contributions to shares that are repurchased from departing employees. That way, the plan would always maintain a 25% level of ownership. If this level of contribution seems inadequate to meet the overall target levels for employee retirement benefits, then additional cash can be contributed to the plan so long as the plan retains most of its investment in company stock.

While this is the simplest approach, it may not be the best one in terms of employee incentives because it limits what can go into the plan to an arbitrary number. A more dynamic approach would be to look at what the company wants to contribute to the plan as a percentage of pay. In most companies with an ESOP used as an incentive plan, there is both an ESOP and a 401(k) plan. Employees can defer pay into the 401(k) plan, and the company may make an additional cash match. The company also contributes a fixed percentage of pay to the ESOP each year, based on a determination of what overall percentage of pay the company should be contributing to the ESOP and 401(k) plan to attract, retain, and motivate employees. In this model, dilution becomes a function of compensation needs. Moreover, as payroll grows, dilution will grow as well. Owners may find that acceptable, however, because the growth usually implies that they now own a smaller piece of a bigger company.

A third approach is to make the determination of how much goes into the ESOP based on profitability or some other performance target. For example, the company might put a percentage of pretax profits into the plan each year. Usually, this percentage is calculated using one of two ways. The first method is to provide an amount that in a normal year the company would consider appropriate and meaningful. The second method is to provide an amount based on an assessment of what seems like an affordable and reasonable percentage of profits to set aside for employees. Here, too, the dilution of other owners will vary. However, because the amount going to employees grows only if the company's profits grow, it is even clearer that the owners will own a smaller part of a larger company.

Whatever approach is chosen, some key issues need to be kept in mind. First, the maximum deductible contribution to the ESOP and other defined contribution plans (401(k), profit sharing, stock bonus, and money purchase plans) is 25% of the eligible pay of plan participants. In leveraged ESOPs in C corporations, the 25% is in addition to contributions to other defined contribution plans or other contributions made to the ESOP for purposes other than repaying the loan. Employee deferrals into the 401(k) plan do not add into this calculation. Second, contributions must be more than symbolic. While research cannot pinpoint a dividing line and say "more than this is enough, and less than this does not work," the average contribution to an ESOP of this type is in the range of 5% to 10% of pay, with many plans above this amount. Third, if the plan is to work as an incentive, employees need to know what they need to do to earn it (if there is a profit sharing formula that triggers it) and what makes the stock price go up and down. As in all ESOP companies, a management style that shares financial information regularly and allows employees structured opportunities to share ideas and information can help achieve this goal.

If the company is an S corporation, another consideration is the required distributions that must be made to the ESOP. Like any other owner, the ESOP must receive a pro-rata share of any distributions. So if the 75% owners get $150,000, the ESOP, with its 25% share, must get $50,000. This is not considered a contribution to the ESOP but rather earnings on ESOP shares. This additional contribution could be used to buy additional company shares, buy back shares from departing employees, or simply as an additional cash contribution to employees. However it is used, it adds to employee accounts and reduces corporate cash flow. In many cases, this will be completely acceptable; in others, it will present a serious issue.

Using the ESOP to Match 401(k) Plan Contributions

Because 401(k) plans require minimum participation levels, companies often match employee payroll deferrals (typically at 25% to 75% of the contribution). The match can be in any number of investment assets the company chooses, including company stock. One way to provide this match is with an ESOP. The ESOP and 401(k) plan can be integrated into a single plan document or can operate side by side. The latter approach is administratively more flexible, although it requires two separate plan documents to be drawn up.

In the simplest approach, the company just contributes stock or cash to buy stock to a nonleveraged ESOP. The contribution may be based on what employees defer, on company profits, or a straight percentage of pay formula. In a more sophisticated approach, the company sets up a leveraged ESOP that borrows money to acquire shares. The allocation of stock from the leveraged ESOP is used to determine the match. For instance, say employees are putting $1 million into the 401(k) from their own deferrals. A leveraged ESOP might acquire 100,000 shares at $20 per share with a 10-year loan and repay 10% of the principal each year. Stock with an original cost of $200,000 per year and $20 per share per year would then be allocated as an employee match in the first year.

But now say that in year two, the stock is worth $25 per share. Now, $250,000 in stock value will be released to employee accounts. If a few years later the stock goes to $50 per share, then $500,000 would be released. Unless payroll deferrals have grown as quickly, employees will be getting a larger match to their 401(k) accounts. The actual cost to the employer will be the same $20 per share, and the amount of the contribution the company records for purposes of contribution limits will also be $20 per share. Accounting rules stipulate that the value declared for the income statement, however, will be the value of the shares when released.

Because the value of the match would vary from year to year with the stock price, the company needs to make some choices about how the match will be made. One way to do this would be to allow the matching amount to vary with the value of the shares. If the share value rose quickly, as happened in many 401(k)/ESOP combinations in the 1990s, employees would see very large matches. If it dropped, the matching amount would fall. Another approach would be to borrow only enough money so that the repayment of principal would release what would normally be expected to be a part of the matching requirement and "top off" the remainder with cash.

Whether the match is leveraged or nonleveraged, the employer needs to decide whether the contribution should literally be a match to what employees defer or just should be a straight contribution. A straight contribution of 3% of pay or more, regardless of how much, if anything, employees defer, has the advantage of automatically qualifying the plan as meeting the testing rules for the 401(k) plan. Aside from solving the discrimination problems, it makes sure everyone gets at least some ownership. By contrast, a match-only approach means stock just goes to those who make wage deferrals, and goes more to those who defer more. Of course, the employer may want to use the ESOP contribution to encourage 401(k) deferrals, in which case this outcome would be precisely what is desired. In some cases, a middle ground will be chosen with a 3% base contribution and the remainder made as an actual match.

Where stock is publicly traded, companies must allow employees to move stock matches to other investments. At least some employees will want to do this, and it may make good financial sense for them to do so. But will this mean too little stock will be retained in the plan? Closely held companies do not face this requirement, but they may want to make it possible for employees to diversify before ESOP rules require it at age 55 with 10 years of service.

One wrinkle of an ESOP/401(k) plan is that companies using the safe harbor matching contribution rule that allows companies to avoid anti-discrimination testing by making minimum contributions to the 401(k) plan must vest the contributions immediately.

Finally, an ESOP/401(k) plan makes it possible for employees to reinvest any dividends paid to them on company stock in a very tax-efficient way. Dividends that employees voluntarily reinvest in company stock are tax-deductible to the employer. While these dividends are normally taxable to the employee, the company can create a dividend switchback program that can provide the equivalent of a pretax dividend. In this approach, the employer designates the payroll department to receive the dividend. The employee has an amount of pay equivalent to the amount of the dividend deferred into a 401(k) plan, and the payroll department increases the amount paid out as salary to the employee by the same amount. This procedure has been approved in many private letter rulings.

Using an ESOP to Acquire New Capital or Other Companies

When Louis Kelso created the ESOP back in the 1950s, his vision was that companies would use it to finance new capital. They would borrow money to buy machinery, buildings, land, and other productive assets that would pay for themselves in extra corporate earnings. By financing the loan through an ESOP, employees would share in the additional ownership value this capital created.

In practice, this has been used less often than Kelso hoped, but it is an important part of many ESOP companies' strategies. Say that a printing company wants to buy a new $500,000 press. Normally, it would borrow the money and deduct the interest. With an ESOP, it would have the ESOP borrow the money (technically, the loan would usually go to the company, which would relend it to the ESOP). The ESOP would use the $500,000 loan to buy new shares in the company, and the company would use the $500,000 to buy the press. The company would then repay the loan by making tax-deductible contributions to the ESOP, thus deducting both principal and interest. As the loan was repaid, shares would be allocated to employee accounts. Other owners would suffer a dilution in terms of the percentage of the company they owned, but if the press proved to be a good investment, the company would gain at least as much in value as was invested (here, $500,000), so the value of their stock would not be any lower, and it could be higher thanks to the tax break and possible additional employee productivity.

Given these advantages, why don't more companies finance capital acquisitions this way? The principal explanation, of course, is that owners would rather keep ownership to themselves. Even though the ESOP could save them some tax money, the tax savings pay for only part of the cost of giving up ownership of the asset. Additional productivity gains are only possible, not guaranteed, and may not make up the difference not accounted for by the tax savings. On the other hand, if a company wants to share ownership anyway, or, especially, if it is already primarily ESOP-owned, then financing capital acquisitions this way can be very attractive.

Buying capital is one way to expand. Buying entire companies is another. The same leveraged approach described above would work to buy another company. But what if the acquiring company is a closely held company that already has an ESOP? Can the acquirer get for the owners of the target company the tax deferral advantage available to other sellers to ESOPs in C corporations?

The answer is that it is possible but requires several extra steps to be taken. These steps are described in detail in the chapter on ESOP financing. Suffice it to say here that the most common approach is the "two-ESOP" approach in which both the target and acquiring company set up ESOPs. Typically, the acquirer will have had an ESOP in place well before the transaction. The target company's owner sells to the newly established target ESOP in a transaction that may be financed by the acquirer and takes Section 1042 treatment. Immediately thereafter, the acquiring company's ESOP merges with the target's ESOP. Typically, the acquiring company's ESOP now owns a majority of the target's shares (because the ESOP in the target had at least a majority). The target company's ESOP participants can now participate in the ESOP of the acquiring company (technically, because the target is a member of acquirer's control group).

At least one or two years later, the two companies actually merge. The delay is necessary to meet tax rules concerning tax-free reorganizations, although there may be specific exemptions for unusual circumstances.

Using an ESOP to Buy Out a Division of Another Company

This application is a variation on the capital acquisition theme. When parent companies are looking to divest divisions or subsidiaries, they often will want to find a synergistic buyer who can offer a premium price. In other cases, however, there either is no such buyer or the company offers to sell to employees, perhaps out of a sense of obligation, to bolster employee morale at other operations, or because of outside pressure.

In these cases, the employees usually form an acquisition company. The company borrows enough money to purchase the assets of the division or subsidiary. At the same time, the new company sets up an ESOP. The company reloans the money it has borrowed to the ESOP, which the ESOP uses to buy shares in the company. The company now takes the loan proceeds and uses them to buy the assets. Alternatively, the ESOP could buy the assets and exchange them for stock. Either way, as the loan is repaid to the ESOP, shares are released to employee accounts.

Structuring the ESOP is the easy part. The real questions in these transactions are feasibility and finance. For the transaction to be feasible, all the usual elements of a sensible business plan must be in place—money, markets, and management. In many spin-off situations, the division or subsidiary may not have developed a management group capable of taking both entrepreneurial and administrative leadership. The new company will also be burdened with a lot of non-productive debt that must be paid fairly quickly. Buyouts are also often hampered by the parent company's desire to compete in similar markets. The sale may be occurring in the first place because the parent does not think much of the markets the division or subsidiary serve. The best candidates, therefore, tend to be operations with solid markets or management whose lines of business are no longer of interest to the parent but whose business prospects are not so stellar as to attract other buyers. Often, there is an identifiable missing piece in these operations, such as bad employee morale, excessive overhead charges by the parent, a lack of parent interest in potentially successful ideas or initiatives from the division or subsidiary, or high labor costs that could be reduced by an ESOP in which employees take concessions. Operations that are simply losing money in depressed markets despite the parent's best efforts are almost never good candidates, while star operations can almost never be bought by employees because someone else will pay more.

The second major hurdle is finance. In most of these buyouts, equity capital is essential. Lenders are not going to lend 100% of the value of a company except in the most unusual circumstances. This equity can take many forms, and often combines a number of elements. Where a great deal of capital is needed, there are specialized investment firms that will purchase a large, usually majority, stake in these companies with the intention of selling to the ESOP over time. Management will almost always be asked to invest its own cash, as much to provide some "skin in the game" to encourage them to stay as to generate capital. High-risk lenders may provide subordinated debt, usually at very high prices. Some states will provide loans or loan guarantees. Parent companies might retain partial ownership or invest in the transaction. Finally, employees will often be asked to contribute, sometimes directly through the purchase of shares and (more often) through wage and benefit concessions.

Buyouts of this kind are expensive to organize, time-consuming, and riskier than other ESOP transactions. They also raise more complicated issues, such as allocating equity between direct investors who risk their own cash and the ESOP, which borrows money on a non-recourse basis on behalf of employees. Few investors will be willing to take a dollar in equity for a dollar in cash if the ESOP gets a dollar in equity for a dollar in borrowed money to be repaid by the company. There are ways to structure these transactions to accommodate everyone's interests, but they take a high level of expertise and can be controversial between the parties involved.

Despite all these issues, when a division or subsidiary is for sale and employees are logical buyers, an ESOP can be a very desirable solution, giving employees a chance to become owners and, in some cases, saving their jobs as well.

Using an ESOP to Save a Failing Company

One of the most publicized, but least common, applications of an ESOP is to save a failing company. Often this will be a division or subsidiary of another company and will follow the scenario above, usually with a strong emphasis on substantial concessions, often in the 10% to 30% range. In other cases, it will be to buy a stand-alone company. The mechanisms for this kind of sale would be similar, but the management problem is usually more acute. Clearly, old management will need to be replaced, so the first issue will be to find out whether there is competent new management willing to enter the picture in what will be a very uncertain new company.

Another scenario is the one followed at a number of airline, steel, and trucking companies in the 1980s and a handful of other companies in the 1990s. Here the employees, often represented by a union, agree to take concessions in return for stock. This was the basic structure of the United Airlines transaction, although United was not in danger of failing (instead, employees saw the danger of the company breaking into four different companies, some of which would pay lower wages). In most of these cases, the plan is time-limited; the ESOP will last only as long as the concessions. During that time, employees typically are given some governance rights, commonly minority representation on the board.

The total buyouts have had a reasonably good track record, given their often dire circumstances; a study by the NCEO in the 1980s found that 60% lasted over five years, and another 20% were sold to other companies. Just 20% closed. Buyouts became much less common in the 1990s, but anecdotally, most seem to still be in business, and some are doing very well. Wage-for-stock deals have fared less well. Most of the companies involved closed within a few years. The ones that survived rarely continued their ESOPs, or like United, froze them so that new employees were not included. More importantly, employers and employees in these companies viewed the plans as temporary, and there were few, if any, efforts to create the kind of ownership culture that can help turn companies around. By contrast, most of the outright buyouts did make such efforts.

Using an ESOP to Bolster the Market for Thinly Traded Shares

Finally, ESOPs can be used to help support trading in thinly traded stocks. By far the most common use of this application is in community banks. These institutions, as well as some other businesses, often have a large number of individual or institutional owners, most of whom own a relatively small percentage of the company. Providing a market for their shares can be difficult. The company can buy back the shares, but it is an after-tax expense. Other owners may want to buy, but only on an occasional basis that will have difficulty matching buyers and sellers. If the stock is traded on the "pink sheets" or a regional stock market, there may not be enough activity to support more than periodic trades. This lack of liquidity will lower the share price to an amount closer to what the price would be if the company were closely held.

An ESOP can, within limits, help solve this problem. The ESOP can use cash reserves from company contributions (remember, companies can contribute cash as well as stock to an ESOP as long as the ESOP remains primarily invested in company stock) or can borrow money to buy stock from owners wanting to sell. This creates liquidity in private companies and strengthens the market in thinly traded public companies. The ESOP cannot be compelled to buy shares, however. The ESOP must determine that the price is fair and that timing of the purchase is appropriate for the best interests of plan participants.

Conclusion

ESOPs are an exceptional vehicle for providing for business continuity, but, as this chapter shows, they have many other applications. It is critical to remember, however, that whatever financial objectives an ESOP is being used to accomplish, it is first and foremost an employee benefit plan. The decision to implement an ESOP, and the way it is subsequently run, must be made with an eye first toward whether the plan is good for employees. As research described elsewhere in this book has shown, plans that are run this way help companies make more money. This added productivity is, in the end, the best reason to use an ESOP.

CHAPTER 5

ESOP Valuation Issues

Corey Rosen

T he law requires that all ESOP transactions involving the stock of the sponsoring employer be based on a current appraisal by an outside, independent valuation expert unless the company's stock is readily tradable on an established securities market. Because most ESOPs are in closely held companies where such independent appraisals are required, valuation is an important issue in the ESOP world. (Public companies with a ready market for their shares do not need a valuation for ESOP purposes; they simply use the market price.)

Who Performs the Valuation

Under the Tax Reform Act of 1986, an outside, independent professional must perform the valuation. There are no standards to determine what constitutes a professional, however, other than a very general requirement found in IRS regulations that they are people who customarily do appraisal work. Appraisers do get certified by various appraisal organizations, but these certifications usually only involve short programs or examinations, not professional degrees or tests of detailed competence. However, appraisers who are chartered financial analysts (CFAs) go through a much more extensive program that requires passing very demanding exams. "Independence" has also not been defined, but most consultants argue it means hiring someone with no other business relationship with the company or another professional performing services for the company. For example, the firm's CPA or an appraiser who is paid by a lawyer who sets up the ESOP would not be independent. Aside from these legal requirements, an appraiser should be sought based on specific ESOP experience.

Some lawyers say that the company should not discuss valuation approaches with an appraiser beforehand because it indicates "appraisal shopping," but most believe the trustee must have a clear idea of what assumptions the appraiser will make in terms of such factors as control premiums, discounts for lack of marketability, the definition of the interest to be valued (a minority, non-marketable interest, for instance), and the repurchase obligation.

The Basic Elements of an Appraisal

An appraiser will look at several factors. These include projected future cash flows and profits, book value, market conditions, debt, management, technology, etc. Data on comparable public companies will be collected, particularly financial ratios such as price/earnings ratios ("P/E ratios"), assets/earnings, and so on. These ratios help determine how much the company being appraised is worth (if comparable public firms have an average 7:1 P/E ratio, for instance, the appraised company could be valued at a similar ratio, adjusting for the typical higher price/earnings ratios found in public companies), but most appraisers also factor in net asset value and/or discounted future cash flow or earnings (that is, how much the right to future revenue streams is worth in terms of a lump sum today). These factors will be blended to come up with a number. Obviously, different appraisers will come up with different values.

From there, the appraiser will adjust the value to reflect discounts for lack of marketability if the company is private (it is harder to sell shares in a private firm than a public firm), lack of control (people pay a premium for control rights), and, for most appraisers, the repurchase obligation. How much, if any, discount is taken varies with the appraiser. For this reason, it is important to discuss these assumptions beforehand. These discounts are discussed in more detail below.

Information the Appraiser Will Need

There are no legal requirements for what must be included in an ESOP valuation. For the valuation to have merit, however, most appraisers will want three to ten years of financial statements, preferably audited or at least reviewed; three to five years of projected financial statements; interim statements as close in time to the valuation as possible; a list of all lines of business, assets, off-balance sheet assets, and liabilities; lists of main customers, suppliers, and competitors; legal agreements affecting the company and its owners (such as by-laws and buy-sell agreements); capital and depreciation expenditure records; major contracts; compensation schedules; a history of any stock sales and offers; and any other information that could affect how much the company is worth.

In addition, the appraiser will want to visit the company and talk to key people. In very complex cases, interviews with customers, suppliers, and industry experts could be in order, but most valuations will not take this step.

Failing to provide adequate information, or providing misleading information in a way that could affect value, is a serious offense that could lead to lawsuits by the participants or the government as well as the loss of tax benefits and the imposition of penalties. ESOP fiduciaries are generally responsible to make sure the valuation consultants receive the proper information.

Factors That Can Reduce Per-Share Value

Control Premiums and Lack of Control Discounts

A control premium is simply the mirror image of a lack of control discount. A shareholder owning less than controlling interest in a company has an investment worth less than a shareholder owning a controlling interest. Controlling shareholders can use the assets much more freely, selling them to other buyers, taking larger or smaller dividends, selecting the strategic direction of the company, etc. In takeover battles in public firms, the run-up in price when an offer is made is usually simply a function of someone offering to pay a premium for control.

Owning a majority of the stock is one level of control, but some issues in companies require more than a majority vote, so shareholders owning enough to block a transaction, but not enough to exercise day-to-day control, may pay a premium for this lower level of control, although not as high a premium as they would pay for majority control. Similarly, an additional premium would be paid for owning enough stock to control all issues.

Just owning shares is not enough, however. Valuation guidelines for ESOPs say that for the ESOP to pay a control premium, the trust must have "control in fact." While this has never been defined in any useful way, it would clearly exclude a situation where the ESOP trustee was controlled by another shareholder. The trustee in that case has only nominal control and should not pay a premium for it.

There is no simple answer as to how much the control premium is worth. Control premiums are often in the range of 25% to 35% but can be higher or lower depending on the level of control involved and how valuable that control is given the assets involved. For instance, a company whose assets are encumbered by long-term covenants (such as with lenders, courts, or regulatory agencies) would have a lower control premium than a company whose assets are not. There is also a lot of variation from one appraisal firm to another.

There is no consensus on whether the ESOP can pay a control premium if it owns a minority position but plans to acquire a control position later. Many valuation consultants say an ESOP can pay a control premium if it has a specific option to buy control in a reasonable time, usually three to five years or less, and obtains an irrevocable proxy to vote a sufficient number of additional shares to take over voting control. Sellers must also agree to provide back-up financing (such as taking a note) if outside financing cannot be found. Others argue this should not be the case, that the ESOP should only pay for control when it acquires it. There is no right or wrong approach, but the valuation process should, in any event, use the same assumptions year after year about control.

If the ESOP already has control, it usually may pay a control price for additional shares if there is an agreement that it will, and if the value is used consistently for all ESOP transactions, including repurchases of shares from employees. Again, however, different appraisers have different philosophies.

Lack of Marketability Discounts

Owners of shares in closely held firms cannot sell their shares as easily as owners of publicly traded ones. Because of that, their shares are worth less. Marketability discounts vary considerably, but they typically range from 10% to 30% in ESOP transactions. Again, the variation is explained by the particular facts (Are there other potential buyers? Is the ESOP a reliable buyer able to make the payments needed to make the purchase?) and differing appraisal philosophies.

Some appraisers argue that the put option in an ESOP reduces or eliminates the marketability discount; others argue it depends on the plan's proven ability to repurchase shares; still others say it depends on whether the contributions to the ESOP needed to repurchase shares increase or decrease what the company would otherwise spend on benefit plans; some appraisers contend that the put option is not the same thing as a liquid market and should provide only a small reduction in the marketability discount. Passionate arguments are made on all sides.

The NCEO has taken a position on this, namely that the put option itself does not create a market unless the company shows it has (or can contribute to the ESOP) the funds to satisfy the put. If that is the case, however, the commitment of these funds to a non-productive purpose should reduce the company's value unless they constitute no more than what would be contributed to employee benefit plans anyway if the ESOP were not in place. Even then, some marketability discount should remain, because the put option is a restricted right to sell shares, subject to all the rules, delays, and limits of the ESOP distribution formula. Not to take this approach, we believe, means the company will overpay for the stock, impeding growth and harming the interests of future employee owners.

A diminishing number of appraisers disagree with this, however, arguing, for instance, that the company could always sell or, in some cases, go public to provide liquidity, or that not to pay the highest price possible is unfair to current participants.

Almost everyone agrees that there is a tendency in valuations to make favorable assumptions up front (such as assuming the put option eliminates the marketability discount) to provide sellers a high price. Trustees need to be very wary of this, however, because it can harm the interests of plan participants down the road.

Liquidity Discounts

This is similar to a marketability discount and is often not taken in closely held firms. It refers to the cost of becoming "liquid" for investors, typically by going public or selling. These transactions involve legal and transactional charges that can add up to 3% to 7% or more of the value of the transaction. Liquidity discounts are not commonly found in valuations where it is assumed that the company will resolve its marketability issues by selling or going public, so the presence of a liquidity discount would often be accompanied by a reduction in the marketability discount.

The Effect of ESOP Debt on Company Value

The debt the ESOP takes on is accounted for as debt of the company. Because the company now has this debt showing up on its balance sheet, its value is reduced. It is generally not reduced, however, by the face value of the debt. For one thing, the ESOP borrowing brings certain tax advantages to the company that should be capitalized and reduce the impact of the debt. Second, the debt is repaid over several years. If the company's earnings exceed the cost of the debt, then the impact of the debt should be discounted to reflect that.

The Impact of the Repurchase Obligation on Value

Until the late 1990s the prevailing view among ESOP appraisers was that the repurchase obligation should not affect the value of ESOP shares. The argument was that the company could always satisfy the obligation by selling. Of course, the large majority of ESOP companies do not want to be sold. The ESOP repurchase obligation represents a significant future cash obligation that can reduce the future free cash flow on which valuations are primarily based.

Since the late 1990s, practitioners and, especially, independent trustees have argued that the repurchase obligation must be considered in setting value. Appraisers should be given repurchase studies as a starting point. The specific methodology that is used to assess the impact varies from appraiser to appraiser, but the general conceptual approach is that appraisers look at the impact on cash flow that would normally accrue with a conventional retirement plan versus the amount that is used both for ongoing ESOP contributions and any additional amounts needed to fund the repurchase. This may be adjusted by available cash in the ESOP trust, whether the company retires or recycles shares, and other factors.

The effect of ignoring the repurchase obligation can be that the company overpays employees leaving sooner and underpays those leaving later. Where share value grows quickly, not adjusting for the cost of this in valuation can also make it difficult to fund the repurchase, possibly forcing the company to sell.

Frequency and Timing of Appraisals

The law requires at least an annual appraisal. The only exception to this is that if there is no stock contribution or benefit distribution in a given year, a full-blown valuation is probably not needed, but the trustee must make a determination that the existing valuation is appropriate. If something significant has changed, then a determination must be made about whether a new appraisal is needed.

Technically, any ESOP transaction or allocation should be at the current appraised value, meaning companies should try to time their ESOP activity with the appraiser's report (buying shares when the report is issued and the trustee determines it represents the fair market value). In practice, this may be impractical in some cases. There are a few ways to deal with this. If the issue is allocating stock, the allocation can be backdated to the determination of value. For instance, imagine the plan year ends in December, as does the fiscal year, and that the valuation is completed March 15. The company can make the allocation in March but credit participant accounts as if the allocation had been made in December at the value that applied to December 31.

If the issue involves a purchase, and the valuation is more than a few weeks old (there is no precise time period), then the trustee should at least certify that there are no material changes in the company or its markets that would cause the ESOP to pay more for the stock than it is currently worth. If the valuation is too conservative, and the ESOP pays less, that is not normally a problem, at least as far as ERISA is concerned. This trustee opinion may require a brief analysis by the appraiser. If conditions have changed materially, however, a new appraisal will be needed.

If shares are distributed under an ESOP a few months after the most recent appraisal, a thorough appraisal (what would be done at least annually in ESOP companies) is not needed, but the trustee must determine whether the old appraisal is valid or can be updated without an appraisal. The trustee must be able to show this is a valid price. Because the fiduciary still is responsible for making sure the price is fair market value, however, not getting an appraisal from an independent appraiser is risky. For instance, how can the trustee decide if a valuation is needed without professional advice? What number would be put on the company's Form 5500 (the plan report annually filed with the government)?

The Effect of Other Equity Investors on an ESOP Valuation

So-called "multi-investor" ESOP transactions raise the difficult issue of "equity allocation." There is no ESOP valuation subject so controversial. The problem can be illustrated by an example. Imagine that a group of employees wants to buy their company. A lender is willing to loan them up to 70% of the asset value of the firm, provided they agree to wage and benefit concessions. This will provide 60% of the asking price. The lender also requires that management put up some of its own money because its wants managers "on the line." That will provide another 10% of the price. The remaining 30% will be obtained from an equity partner, perhaps another company or private investors who are willing to put up cash.

The valuation problem is to assess how much each investor should get. The simple view would be "dollar for dollar." The ESOP is putting up 60%, so it should get 60%, while the managers get 10%, and the investors get 30%. The cash investors will argue, however, that they are putting their assets at risk; the ESOP will repay its debt out of future earnings, and the participants in the plan will not be liable if there are losses. The employees argue that they are taking concessions and that the ESOP provides important tax benefits as well.

In the 1980s, some leveraged ESOPs were put together in which equity investors got a different class of stock that provided them with much more ownership for fewer dollars, relative to the ESOP purchase. The Department of Labor took legal action to challenge some of these, arguing for the "dollar for dollar" approach. That position made multi-investor ESOPs virtually impossible to put together; investors wanted more for an investment with those kinds of risks. Over time, some approaches to this problem have been developed that use convertible preferred stock for the ESOP, allowing it to pay a higher price for its interest in the company than other investors, or providing investors with stock warrants (the right to buy additional shares at a fixed price in return for buying some shares at market price), or stock options.

The particular valuation techniques used to allocate equity involve assessing comparable rates of return for investments of similar risk, capitalizing the value of future ESOP tax benefits and/or employee concessions, and complex mathematical models to assess the present value of income streams to various investors.

Valuations vs. Fairness Opinions

A valuation assesses either the fair market value of an enterprise or of the ESOP share of the enterprise, depending on its purpose. A fairness opinion determines the fairness of a transaction to participants in the transaction. In simple transactions, this is not an issue. Where there are multiple owners, and especially where there are different classes of stock or different groups are putting up different kinds of investments (one group cash, one group borrowing money, an ESOP borrowing money the company repays, employees putting up wage or benefit concessions, etc.), fairness is more complicated. If one investor puts in $1 million in cash and the ESOP puts in $1 million with borrowed money to be repaid out of future earnings, what is a fair price for both to pay? These and similar situations call for a professional financial advisor to opine on the fairness of the transaction, but the ESOP trustee must ultimately make the decision. Fairness opinions are not legally required in ESOP or other transactions but are highly advisable in complex ones.

With a fairness opinion, a financial advisor is retained to advise the ESOP fiduciary to determine if the offer to buy stock is fair to all parties. The advisor will assess present and future prospects for the company, the existence of other alternatives to the sale, the ability to obtain financing for the transaction, and the overall effect of the proposal on the company's various constituencies. The report may just be a letter with an opinion, outlining the methods used to arrive at the judgment.

Cost and Contracts

It is important to note that the appraiser is hired by and reports to the trustee, not the company. The appraisal is done to protect the ESOP, not maximize the sale price for the owner(s). Nonetheless, it is the company that will pay the fee. Initial appraisals will typically run $10,000 to $15,000 in conventional transactions; more complex transactions (such as with multiple investors or multiple lines of business) will cost more. Repeat appraisals will be less costly, typically two-thirds to half the initial cost.

CHAPTER 6

Financing an ESOP

Corey Rosen

E SOPs can be a very appealing way to transfer ownership to employees, but they can do that only if the ESOP can come up with a way to acquire the shares. In the simplest model, the company can fund an ESOP by contributing shares directly to the plan. That provides a good employee benefit, but most ESOPs are used to buy out one or more owners or for business expansion. To do that, the ESOP needs a source of cash. Many people we talk to approach ESOPs with the assumption that this can (or maybe should) come directly from employees, whether through direct purchases or moving other retirement plan assets into the ESOP. While this is possible, it is complicated and expensive to do, and it may impose more risk on employees than employees should or are willing to take on. Instead, ESOPs are financed primarily in one of three ways:

1. The company makes periodic cash contributions to the ESOP to enable it to buy shares.

2. The company borrows money from an outside lender, then re-loans it to the ESOP. The company contributes cash to the ESOP to repay the loan.

3. The ESOP takes a note from the seller or sellers, again with the company putting cash into the plan to repay the debt.

This chapter draws significantly on Mary Josephs and Neal Hawkins, "ESOP Underwriting Considerations," chapter 7 in Leveraged ESOPs and Employee Buy-outs, *6th ed. (NCEO, 2013), and Kenneth E. Serwinski, "Financing the Leveraged ESOP," chapter 4 in* Selling Your Business to an ESOP *(NCEO, 2012).*

If one or a combination of these three methods is insufficient, then the company may seek outside investors who will purchase some of the stock or purchase equity rights, such as warrants, to complete the deal.

This chapter looks at the various approaches to ESOP financing. While we cover the basic practices, there are many variations on these approaches. Creative lenders and advisors may be able to come up with alternative approaches. The chapter is organized as follows:

- Financing ESOPs without using debt
- Mechanics of ESOP debt financing
- Uses for ESOP debt
- Bank financing
- Seller financing
- Mezzanine financing and bond markets
- Equity investments

It is important to note at the outset that ESOPs are not a magic wand to raise money. Companies that do not have solid financials, or very good reasons to think that they will produce them in the immediate future, are rarely good ESOP financing candidates, any more than they are good candidates for any other kind of financing.

Financing ESOPs Without Using Debt

By far the simplest way to finance an ESOP is for the company to make cash contributions to the plan, which the plan then uses to buy company stock. These contributions can be for up to 25% of the eligible pay of plan participants in both S and C ESOPs. If the company has other defined contribution plans, company (but not employee) contributions to these plans will reduce this percentage dollar for dollar. Within these limits, the contributions are fully deductible.

This approach works well for companies looking to buy one or more owners out over time. It also works well if the company prefers not to borrow money, does not have the debt capacity, or wants to fund the ESOP on the basis of annual profits rather than paying a fixed amount as required by debt repayments.

The disadvantage of this approach is that many owners want to take advantage of the Section 1042 tax deferral options available to owners of closely held C corporation shares. To qualify, the ESOP must own 30% or more of the company's stock. Even contributing at the maximum percentages, it could take some years before reaching this level. One alternative is for a company that knows it will want to buy out an owner in the future to contribute cash to the plan but not use it to buy shares until there is enough to buy 30% of the stock. While an ESOP must, by law, be "primarily" invested in company stock, most advisors agree that if the plan states that the intention is to invest in company stock when enough cash is available to reach the 30% level, and that this will occur within two or three years, the IRS will not object (and, indeed, we are not aware of there having been any objections, even in plans that did not buy stock for a longer period of time). It would be advisable in these circumstances to provide the ESOP trustee with a right of first refusal to purchase any shares offered for sale and an option to buy shares once the 30% threshold is met.

In some cases, companies will accumulate cash over one or two years, then borrow the remaining amount to get to the 30% level or whatever level is desired. Once a company does have a loan, it can also make additional cash contributions to the plan. For instance, a company may borrow a conservative amount with the intention of making additional contributions if earnings allow.

Mechanics of ESOP Debt Financing

About three-quarters of ESOPs are funded with borrowing. A variety of rules apply to these loans. In almost all ESOP loans, the lender loans money to the company (the "outside" loan), which the company then reloans to the ESOP (the "inside" loan). While the lender could loan directly to the ESOP, the only collateral the ESOP can offer is the stock itself and any earnings on the shares acquired by the loan. The lender wants a better source of collateral than that. The outside and inside loans do not have to have the same terms. The internal loan must meet the fiduciary standards for ESOPs, however. Two issues are paramount here. First, the loan rate must be an "arm's-length equivalent," generally meaning it would have to be no higher than the external loan rate. Second, while the term can be longer, the fiduciaries must be able to show that extending the loan is for the benefit of plan participants. The most typical application of this would be when loan repayments on the terms of the external loan would exceed the maximum allowable amounts that can be added to employee accounts each year. By extending the term of the inside loan, the company is able to fund the ESOP; otherwise, either it would have no plan at all or the ESOP would have to acquire fewer shares, either of which would arguably not be in the interests of employees. In other cases, the loan limits are not a problem, but the company wants to spread the ESOP benefit over a longer period of time. For instance, the company may be repaying the outside loan over five years, which would translate into 25% of eligible pay each year (or more if dividends and distributions are used).

Each year, as the loan is repaid, a percentage of shares held in the ESOP trust equal to the percentage of the loan that has been repaid that year is released from what is called "the ESOP suspense account." The shares are then allocated to employee participant accounts based on the company's allocation formula (such as relative eligible pay). In C companies, tax-deductible dividends can also be used to repay an ESOP loan, as can distributions in an S corporation. S corporation distributions are not tax-deductible, however. The dividends or distributions paid on allocated shares must release a number of unallocated shares with a value at least equal to the dividend or distribution. Distributions or dividends on unallocated shares would release the number of shares paid for. If the share value has fallen from the purchase, this means more shares than are being paid for in terms of the loan payment must be released. For distributions or dividends paid on allocated shares, the company must release unallocated shares based on relative share balances of participants; for dividends or distributions paid on unallocated shares, the shares can be allocated either on relative share balances or the company's normal allocation formula.

The company can use one of two formulas to calculate the percentage of the loan that has been repaid: the "principal-only method" or the "principal-and-interest method." The principal-only method releases the percentage of the shares that is equal to the percentage of the total principal paid. This method cannot be used unless the payments of principal and interest on the loan are no less rapid than level annual payments of principal and interest over a 10-year loan, using standard amortization tables to determine allowable interest rates. The principal-and-interest method releases shares based on the following formula:

$$
\begin{array}{l}
\text{Number of} \\
\text{shares to be} \\
\text{released and} \\
\text{allocated}
\end{array}
=
\begin{array}{l}
\text{Number of} \\
\text{shares in} \\
\text{account before} \\
\text{release}
\end{array}
\times
\dfrac{\text{Principal and interest payments}}{\text{for the year}}{\text{Principal and interest payments}}
$$

Number of shares to be released and allocated	=	Number of shares in account before release	×	Principal and interest payments for the year
				Principal and interest payments remaining on the loan, including those for the current year

The number of shares held in the suspense account just before the release is multiplied by a fraction, the numerator of which is the principal and interest payments for the year and the denominator of which is the principal and interest payments remaining on the loan, including the current year. In other words, shares are allocated based on the total amount of the remaining loan (principal and interest) paid that year. The number of years on the loan must be fixed, not variable; renewal or extensions of the loan cannot be considered; and the interest rate is the rate that applies at the end of the year involved. The principal-only method releases shares more slowly, in most cases, and is often preferred by banks.

The contribution limits for leveraged ESOPs depend on whether the company is a C or S corporation. As discussed in chapter 1 under "Limitations on Contributions," there are two limits to consider: the amount the company can contribute to the plan (and other defined contribution plans) overall and the maximum annual addition to any one employee's account. The amount of the principal repaid is used to calculate the value of the employer contribution for the "annual addition" calculation. If the stock value rises, this means the amount added to an employee's account will be greater than the amount the company paid for the shares that is used for purposes of the limitation calculations. The IRS also allows companies to use the value of the shares released, however, if the share value is lower. Companies must choose to use the method in advance and use it on a consistent basis.

In C corporations, the total company contribution limit is 25% of eligible pay to repay the principal each year. (As chapter 1 notes, this can be counted separately from other contributions to an ESOP and other defined contribution plans.) Interest payments and reallocated forfeitures do not count in any of the C corporation limitation calculations provided that not more than one-third of the allocated benefits do not go to "highly compensated employees," as that term is defined by the law. Companies can also pay "reasonable" dividends on ESOP shares to go beyond this limit. "Reasonable" has not been specifically defined but should not be much in excess of what similar companies might pay on similar earnings. This limit is not affected by contributions to other defined contribution plans. No one participant can receive more than 100% of eligible pay in one year as an annual addition, or $52,000 (as of 2014), whichever is less.

S corporation rules are more limiting. Interest payments and forfeitures do count toward the 25% of pay limitation. Distributions on shares can be used to go above the limits, but, as noted above, they are not tax-deductible.

Note that the leverage will have an effect on company value. After the loan, the price per share will decline. While the decline may not be dollar-for-dollar with the size of the loan (primarily because of ESOP tax benefits), it will reduce the value the stock would have had without the leverage until the loan is repaid. Very successful ESOP companies may see their stock recover quickly if employee productivity goes up, but this is not predictable or reliable. This effect is especially important in two circumstances: when there are other non-ESOP owners and in second-stage ESOP transactions.

Non-ESOP owners may be distressed to see that the sale of stock by their partners has hurt their stock value. Some companies have the owners sell pro-rata to deal with this; in other cases, the problem is avoided because the other owners are not looking to sell right away anyway.

In second-stage ESOP transactions, existing employees see the value of their accounts decline. For employees who may receive a distribution before the loan is repaid, this can be painful. Some companies deal with this by providing a floor-price guarantee for the shares until the loan is repaid. That needs to be properly structured to avoid potential fiduciary issues.

Using Preferred or Super-Common Stock

In some transactions, the ESOP will purchase preferred shares rather than common. In an ESOP, preferred shares must be convertible to common at the option of the fiduciary. Preferred stock receives preference over common should the company be liquidated or go into bankruptcy and normally receives higher dividends than any class of common. It may or may not have voting rights. Because it receives a higher dividend (a current payment of company earnings), it gets less of the company's future equity value (a deferred payment of earnings, in effect). As a result of this, it tends to go up and down in value less than common. Fiduciaries need to obtain advice from valuation advisors on appropriate pricing and conversion ratios for the preferred. Super-common stock is much like preferred, having special dividend rights but not necessarily liquidation rights.

A common reason a company would choose preferred is because it would allow the sellers to receive a higher price per share, letting them sell a smaller percentage of the company to reach the same financial goal. Preferred and super-common are also used when there are equity investors in a leveraged ESOP transaction. The use of preferred for the ESOP allows the equity investors to buy common shares at a relatively lower value than would otherwise be possible. This may be important because the equity investors often do not want to pay the same price as the ESOP, given that they are putting their own assets at risk while the ESOP is only putting the shares it acquires at risk. The fiduciary rules on allocating equity between the ESOP and equity investors can be tricky; this is one common solution to the problem.

Uses for ESOP Debt

Most ESOP loans are used to buy out one or more owners of closely held companies. The ESOP uses the borrowed funds to buy shares from the owner(s), who, if they qualify, may elect the Section 1042 tax deferral and invest in qualified replacement property (see the chapter on selling to an ESOP in a closely held company for details). ESOPs can also be used to acquire new capital, buy other companies, or refinance existing debt.

When an ESOP is used to acquire new capital, the company issues new shares and sells them to the ESOP, which borrows money to purchase the shares. The company takes the proceeds of the sale and buys the new machinery, real estate, intellectual property, or other investment. The loan is then repaid in pretax dollars by making contributions to the ESOP. ESOP creator Louis Kelso actually envisioned this as the primary application of ESOPs, although in practice it is used only occasionally. The same technique could be used to refinance existing debt.

A more common application is to use the ESOP to buy another company. The structure here is somewhat complicated, but many

ESOP companies, especially 100% S corporation ESOPs (i.e., S corporations wholly owned by their ESOPs) that have paid off their initial acquisition debt, are now doing this. In the most common approach, the target company is either a C corporation or an S corporation that converts to C status. This allows the seller to elect the Section 1042 tax deferral on the sale. To meet IRS rules that make this transaction favorably taxed, a "two-ESOP" structure is commonly used.

Typically, the acquirer will have had an ESOP in place well before the transaction. The target company sets up an ESOP. The target company's owner then sells to the ESOP in a transaction that may be financed by the acquirer and takes Section 1042 tax-deferral treatment by reinvesting in qualified replacement property. Immediately thereafter, the acquiring company's ESOP merges with the target's ESOP. Typically, the acquiring company's ESOP would now own a majority of the target's shares (because the ESOP in the target had at least a majority), so that the target company ESOP participants can now participate in the ESOP of the acquiring company because the target is a member of acquirer's control group.

The details of this approach are beyond this book; our book *Selling Your Business to an ESOP* explains this and other approaches commonly used.

A 100% S corporation ESOP may also simply borrow money to buy the target, not attempting to get the seller tax-deferral treatment. The employees of the target would then commonly become participants in the ESOP. Because a 100% S corporation ESOP does not pay federal, or usually state, income tax, it would not be concerned about maximizing its own tax benefits by using the ESOP to take on the debt.

Bank Financing

ESOP companies often borrow money from banks, although seller financing has become much more common in recent years. Less often, ESOPs borrow from mezzanine lenders or the bond market.

Traditional ESOP financing is accomplished with senior credit from a bank. Banks do not receive any special incentives to loan to ESOPs but may be more receptive to ESOPs because their tax benefits can enhance the borrower's cash flow. Most banks are not familiar with ESOPs, however, and some may not want to make such a loan. In general, however, companies that have feasible transactions do not have difficulty finding lenders.

Banks will make the same kinds of assessments of loan quality they do with any transaction acquiring non-productive debt. They will focus on the "four c's": capital, character (management and credit history), collateral, and cash flow. In some cases, to assure that key management remains committed to the transaction, and/or to provide some additional up-front equity, lenders may require managers to make an investment. In some cases, that will be a purchase of common stock; in others (especially 100% S corporation ESOPs), it will be for some kind of stock right.

Looking at cash flow, a lender will want to have a ratio generally between 1.25 and 1.75 times the debt obligation. This is a general range, and it will vary up or down depending on economic circumstances and how aggressive the particular lender is. The bank will also want to be sure that the company can add additional debt to finance operations, if needed.

Collateral presents a potentially trickier issue. As noted, banks are not interested in having the ESOP stock as collateral. If the loan is to purchase another company or invest in new assets, this will serve as the primary collateral, but the bank will probably discount the value of the asset and seek additional coverage. If the loan is to purchase existing shares, the bank will seek collateral both from company assets and, preferably, from the seller. In many ESOP transactions, the seller reinvests in qualified replacement property, which the bank will seek as collateral. Sellers will want to negotiate a reduction in this collateral obligation as the loan is repaid. There are many variations on how this is done, such as accelerating the release if the company's EBIDTA exceeds a certain level. All of this is a matter of negotiation, however.

In assessing corporate collateral, various assets will be discounted differently. Accounts receivable, for instance, might be discounted only 20%, while inventory and the book value of fixed assets might be discounted 50%.

It is important to understand the effect of the ESOP on the company's balance sheet. The ESOP shows up as corporate debt. When the debt is recorded on the balance sheet, an equal and offsetting debit is recorded in the equity section as a "contra-equity account." It has to appear here because the ESOP loan does not show up as an asset in the asset section (although if the company is using the loan to buy a productive asset, that asset will appear on the asset side). This contra-equity account is eliminated as the ESOP debt is paid. The amount of the release is equal to the number of shares released from the ESOP suspense account and allocated to participants. Because of the way this process works, the amount by which the contra-equity account is reduced will not necessarily equal the amount by which the debt is reduced. Banks will use this ESOP-adjusted balance sheet number to calculate coverage ratios. In some cases, this accounting procedure could result in a negative number, which could raise legal issues for lenders under fraudulent conveyance laws. Companies need to work closely with lenders to make sure they understand how ESOP accounting works. When they do understand it, experience indicates they may be more willing to go beyond normal coverage ratios.

Some of the specific financial measures and ratios lenders look for include cash flow (requiring a minimum of EBITDAE—earnings before interest, taxes, depreciation, amortization, and employee benefit expense), debt service coverage (the ratio of EBITDAE to all required payments to the lender), leverage (senior debt to EBITDAE), interest coverage (EBITDAE to interest expense), and fixed charge coverage (EBITDAE to fixed charges). Again, all this is something that is negotiated and varies from transaction to transaction.

Banks will also usually place certain covenants on the loan. For instance, in a C corporation they may require that dividends, if issued, only be used to repay the ESOP debt. In an S corporation, they may require any distributions paid to the ESOP to be used for the same purpose, rather than just added to employee accounts. They may also require that the company not start repurchasing shares, except as legally required for retirement, death or disability, until the loan is repaid. This is allowable in C corporations, but it appears that it is not in S corporations because the law does not specifically state that S corporations are eligible for this deferral of distribution to terminated employees. Audited financial statements are also usually required. There may also be restrictions on bonuses, compensation, and capital expenditures.

Because of all the bank requirements, it is very difficult, and usually impossible, for an ESOP to buy 100% of a company in a single transaction financed by a bank. Instead, most ESOPs proceed in a series of steps to reach the final percentage ownership goal or, if they want to go 100% in one transaction, rely on seller financing.

The term of an ESOP loan is typically 5 to 7 years, and rarely longer than 10 years. This is for the "outside" loan; provided an extension of the inside loan is judged by the ESOP fiduciary to be in the best interests of plan participants, the loan can be longer. Loan terms more than 10 years should be considered carefully, however. It may be prudent in these cases, for instance, to allow distributions of allocations to start at some point after the outside loan is repaid but before the inside loan is.

Seller Financing

More and more ESOP transactions are being funded by sellers taking a note. In some cases, the seller financing is in addition to bank financing, in which case it is usually subordinated to it. Usually, seller financing is structured with the outside-inside loan structure described above. The seller has the company repay the note; the company loans the money to the ESOP. The added flexibility this provides may be especially important in seller financing. For instance, if the company is experiencing difficulties, the seller might forgive a loan payment or accept interest only; this would be possible, but more complicated, with an ESOP loan. The terms of the loan to the ESOP should be arms-length equivalents (similar to terms for a bank loan) or more favorable to the ESOP.

Seller financing has become more popular for four reasons. First, it is simpler to leave the bank and all its legal and financial requirements out of the picture. Especially if the bank is requiring qualified replacement property as collateral, the seller may see little difference in the risk between a bank loan and a seller note. Second, in the past, C corporation owners wanting to defer taxes found seller notes made the process difficult, for reasons explained below. But now techniques are available to solve this problem. In any event, with relatively low capital gains taxes (which, however, increased in 2013 for high-income taxpayers), many owners have not wanted to take advantage of the Section 1042 tax deferral, even if they qualify, while other owners cannot because their company is an S corporation, and they do not want to convert to a C. Third, bank restrictions on the amount of leverage a company can take out mean that the percentage of the company that the ESOP can buy can be limited. Finally, in today's market, many owners find that the interest rate on the note is an attractive investment relative to other possibilities.

There are, however, drawbacks to seller financing. If the company defaults, the seller gets the company back. Sellers may need to stay more involved with the company as a result, often insisting on covenants similar to banks, as well as a board role, to protect their interests. Second, if the seller does want to defer taxation on the gain, the techniques available are somewhat more limiting in terms of investment strategies. Finally, for all their requirements, bank loans do impose a rigorous process of analysis to make sure an ESOP loan really is feasible.

Using Seller Financing When the Seller Wants to Defer Taxation on the Gain

If a seller loans to an ESOP, he or she may be not be able to take full advantage of the Section 1042 tax deferral, which allows them to defer tax by reinvesting in other securities. The law specifies that a seller to an ESOP has 12 months after the sale and 3 months before it to reinvest the proceeds in securities of qualifying companies. In a seller-financed transaction, the seller may be getting paid in annual installments. The seller cannot just reinvest these installments as he or she receives them and qualify. Instead, only the amount actually reinvested during the 15-month period qualifies. As a result, the seller must have other funds to reinvest within the reinvestment period to make this work.

There are, however, techniques that make this possible. The seller would first take out a loan from a bank to buy a long-term non-callable bond that qualifies as replacement property (these special securities are called "ESOP Notes" and can be found through your advisors). Generally, banks will loan for up to 90% of the face value of these bonds because they are so secure. Then the seller uses the proceeds of the ESOP note to repay the loan to the bank. The bond interest rate is usually low, just somewhat above the London Interbank Offered Rate (LIBOR). The loan from the bank would carry a higher interest rate, but the ESOP note would probably carry a still higher rate because of its added risk.

There are a number of long-term (30- to 60-year) non-callable bonds specially designed for the ESOP rollover investment. Because they are non-callable (the issuer cannot buy them back at its discretion), the buyer can feel secure that they can be held until death without triggering a "disposition," as a call would be considered, and having to pay tax. The ESOP Note, as it is repaid, can usually be borrowed against to generate cash. The borrowed funds can then be used to buy and sell whatever the buyer wants. The buyer pays tax when these investments are sold, but only based on their increase in value.

This strategy may or may not be attractive. As noted, the long-term bonds typically pay a variable rate lower than other long-term interest rates. The loan interest rate to buy the bond is often somewhat higher than the bond interest rate (the loan rate is usually fixed, so its relationship to the bond interest rate varies, but it would typically start at a point or so higher). The seller can partially offset this low-return investment by borrowing against the bond as the loan is repaid to buy higher-yielding investments. Contrast that with using the proceeds of a bank loan to invest in whatever portfolio of qualified property the seller chooses and holding on to that portfolio long term, or buying an ESOP Note with cash up front and borrowing up to 90% of it to buy and sell other investments right away.

Of course, all this matters only if the seller cares about the tax deferral. If that is not the case, the seller just pays capital gains tax on the proceeds of the seller-financed sale and does whatever he or she wants with the money. The seller, 25% owners, and family member can then all be in the ESOP, something that is not the case if the tax deferral is chosen. Moreover, the Section 1042 tax deferral is available only to sellers in C corporations.

Mezzanine Financing and Bond Markets

The large majority of ESOP transactions rely on senior credit or seller financing without any additional financing. In some cases, however, this is not sufficient to buy as many shares as the sellers desire to sell. In others, lenders may require some equity investment, employees may want to buy shares, or the sellers may insist that management purchase into the transaction.

If additional debt is needed, mezzanine lenders would often be sought. Mezzanine debt is subordinate to senior credit and therefore carries a higher (sometimes much higher) interest rate, often in the 20% to 30% range. These lenders may also want the right to convert some of the debt to equity. For instance, a loan might be structured so that part of it is repaid as straight debt and part as an equity claim that kicks in at a defined future point, either in years or when a certain target is met. In these cases, companies should negotiate for a lower interest rate than would be the case with straight debt. The equity conversion feature can also be structured so that the lender sells the conversion right back to the company before ever actually acquiring shares (such as would typically be the case with a warrant). Mezzanine lenders are typically investment firms. Your banker or attorney may be able to help locate these providers, but larger transactions might require the services of an investment banker. Investment bankers place financing with private sources, charging a percentage of the financing as a fee.

The bond market is another alternative, but it is practical only for very large transactions. Historically, very few ESOP transactions have sought financing from the private bond market. Placing these bonds requires an investment banker, a "road show" to sell the offering, and compliance with securities rules.

In rare cases, state or local governments may also provide financing or financial guarantees. Most often, states or local government will get involved only where there is potential significant job loss and sufficient private financing cannot be found. Governments may subordinate their position on the loans but not charge mezzanine debt rates, or they may act as a guarantor of a loan. Over the last two decades, however, there have probably only been a few dozen instances of government involvement. The federal Small Business Administration can also provide loan guarantees for ESOPs for relatively small loans, an ability rarely sought or used by ESOP companies.

Equity Investments

Outside Investors

If outside equity investment is needed, ESOPs can look to all the same sources any company can, such as institutional investors, specialized private equity firms, venture capitalists, "angel" investors (individuals looking to make investments in higher-yielding ventures), and friends and family.

Equity investment in ESOPs poses some special challenges, however. Many equity investors would argue that because the ESOP is buying shares with a non-recourse loan, while they are buying shares with their own money, more shares per dollar invested should be allocated to the equity investors. The U.S. Department of Labor, however, has not agreed with this approach. Advisors have come up with various ways to create fairer ways to allocate equity in these deals, but companies seeking to do this need to seek highly experienced professional advice. In general, outside investors in an ESOP prefer mezzanine debt to actual equity, partly because of the limitations on how multi-investor transactions with an ESOP can be structured. Whatever technical solutions are found, however, ESOP equity investors have to understand that the ESOP fiduciary is required to negotiate the best possible deal for the ESOP. This added uncertainty has made it more difficult for ESOPs to find outside equity partners, although certainly not impossible.

Employee Investors

A more available source is management. Banks occasionally require management to buy into a deal, while in other cases managers either want to invest or sellers require it. The same fiduciary rules apply to their investment as outside equity investors. In our experience, however, managers usually buy in to ESOP transactions at the same price as the ESOP, not seeking any special treatment. Where managers do buy in, they would usually end up with somewhere between 5% and 20% of the shares sold. These investments must come from after-tax dollars. Companies can loan the money to managers, but interest rates not considered at arms-length terms are taxable. Managers can also purchase equity rights, such as stock appreciation rights or phantom stock. Both need to have fair values set by an appraiser to comply with fiduciary rules. Both approaches also need to comply with deferred compensation taxation rules, although this should not present any difficulties for properly drafted plans.

Employees more generally can also become investors. In rare cases, employees have been asked to purchase shares individually. While this is possible, it is often impractical. Companies must comply with securities law requirements. Offers to sell 15% of the equity of a company in a 12-month period can receive an exclusion from costly and burdensome securities registration rules, but substantial financial disclosure will be required. If the company has more than $10 million in assets and the sale results in 2,000 or more total owners of the company, or 500 or more owners who are "unaccredited investors" (the ESOP only counts as one investor, however), then the company is *de facto* a public company and subject to securities laws. Shares received from employee compensation plans in transactions exempt from securities registration (such as those under Rule 701) are not included in the calculation of owners. Moreover, employees must use after-tax money to make the purchases, and the amounts that can be raised often do not justify the costs and risks involved.

More common would be to use existing retirement plan assets, typically money in 401(k) plans or profit sharing plans. Most 401(k) plans have two parts: the part made up of employer matches and the part made up of employee contributions. The considerations for the employer match part would be exactly the same as the considerations for moving profit sharing assets. One way to move profit sharing or employer 401(k) contribution funds would be for the plan's fiduciary unilaterally to decide to do so. The problem here is that the funds in either plan are invested in a diversified portfolio, while in the ESOP they will be in a single investment. If that investment does poorly, or even fails to do as well as a prudently created portfolio would, the fiduciary may be sued for misusing employee assets. For employee deferral funds, this unilateral decision is far too risky for a fiduciary to make.

To avoid this fiduciary risk, some companies give employees a choice about whether to move some or all of their account balances into the ESOP. The first potential problem this creates is that not enough funds may be moved. The second is that the employees are making an investment decision in doing this. Securities law is unclear on whether this requires a registration if the various securities law exemptions (most commonly offering less than 15% of equity) are not met, although it does appear that a one-time-only offering may be excluded. Even if registration is not required, however, full and objective financial disclosure certainly is. That can be an expensive process. It also requires the disclosure of executive salaries and other data the company may not want to make available. Finally, there is an issue about whether it is advisable, even by means of holding an election, to encourage employees to move diversified assets into company stock, especially if those diversified assets represent a significant part of their retirement.

Most ESOP advisors, therefore, recommend that at most 15% to 30% of profit sharing assets or employer contributions to a 401(k) be moved to an ESOP by a fiduciary, and then only with appropriate advice from independent financial experts certifying that the ESOP is a good investment. Where employees are making the choice, the percentage can be much larger, but most advisors urge companies to limit the percentage employees can move except in very unusual circumstances.

Conclusion

ESOP financing is really not all that different from any kind of corporate financing. All the same techniques can be used. Unlike conventional financing, however, ESOPs can add the unique tax benefit of allowing borrowers to deduct the principal on the loan, something that can be done no other way. A $5 million loan might normally require a company to generate around $8 million in pretax earnings to repay the principal; an ESOP only requires $5 million. In return for this special benefit, however, ESOPs must meet specific rules to assure the plan operates for the benefit of plan participants. This will add complexity to the transaction, but with the advice of experienced professionals, most companies that are willing to share ownership broadly and that have solid financial prospects will find practical ways to finance their plans.

CHAPTER 7

ESOP Distribution and Diversification Rules

Scott Rodrick

Distributing ESOP benefits is a central responsibility and function of the plan, and it raises many issues. There are a number of interlocking rules that apply to various facets of distributions. This chapter covers the main rules. It also covers diversification, which offers ESOP participants nearing retirement the opportunity to diversify their ESOP investment by moving part of their account balance out of company stock; one way this can be accomplished is by distributing the amount to be diversified.

Companies have a certain amount of flexibility in how they may structure their distribution policies and may be more generous than the law demands them to be (for example, not delaying distributions as long as is legally permissible). However, it is important to remember that the ESOP plan document (which must adhere to the rules, such as those set forth here) controls, and that if the plan document does not authorize a particular thing the company wants to do with respect to distribution, then the company cannot do it. Therefore, the company and its ESOP attorney (and possibly other consultants) should discuss these matters and make the appropriate plan design decisions before the ESOP attorney drafts the plan and the company establishes its ESOP. A company may modify at least some of the

The author thanks Karen Ng of Nixon Peabody LLP for her assistance in preparing this chapter.

distribution options in a nondiscriminatory manner (e.g., it cannot treat similarly situated participants in a different manner), but it is not always clear what is permissible.

The Special ESOP Rules

ESOP benefits are mainly paid to participants after their employment with the company terminates, whether because of retirement or other reasons. There are two sets of rules that govern the main ESOP distribution issues: the special ESOP rules and the general rules that apply to all qualified plans such as ESOPs. Section 409(o) of the Internal Revenue Code (the "Code"), enacted in 1986, sets forth the special ESOP rules, which apply to distributions attributable to stock acquired by the ESOP after 1986.

Retirement, Death, or Disability vs. Other Terminations

As far as how soon benefits are paid, the special ESOP rules distinguish between *retiring* (or death or disability) on the one hand, and simply *leaving* the company due to other reasons (such as quitting or being fired) on the other hand. When a participant attains the normal retirement age under the plan, becomes disabled, or dies, the ESOP must begin to distribute vested benefits[1] during the plan year following the event (unless the ESOP plan document permits the participant to elect to defer receipt of the distribution). When employment terminates for other reasons, however, the beginning of distribution may be, and often is, delayed for some time. It must start no later than the sixth plan year after the plan year in which termination occurred (unless the participant is re-employed by the same company before then, the ESOP plan document permits the participant to elect to defer receipt of the distribution, or the rule stated below on delaying distributions of leveraged shares applies).

---

1. Note that under Code Section 411(a), a participant must become 100% vested upon reaching "normal retirement age" as defined in the Code.

Lump-Sum vs. Installments

Under the special ESOP rules, distributions may be made in a lump sum, in installments, or in a combination of a lump sum and installments. Installment distributions must be substantially equal in size, must be made not less frequently than annually, and must take place over a period no longer than five years. This actually means six annual payments, not five: for example, a distribution beginning in 2014 and ending in 2019 (i.e., five years later) will have payments in 2014, 2015, 2016, 2017, 2018, and 2019. However, this five-year period may be extended an additional year (up to a maximum of five additional years) for each $210,000 or fraction thereof by which a participant's benefit exceeds $1,050,000 (as of 2014; these figures are indexed by the IRS for cost-of-living adjustments).

This means an employee may have to wait a long time to receive benefits. Take someone who becomes 100% vested in his or her ESOP benefit and then quits: he or she may have to wait five years[2] until distributions begin (assuming this period is not further delayed by waiting for an ESOP loan to be repaid, as described below), then another five years of installments, and, in the case of a large account balance as described in the paragraph above, up to yet another five years to receive distribution of the entire ESOP benefit. However, most participants do not have to wait that long. A 2005 survey by the NCEO found that 93.1% of all ESOPs paid out in full within one year of death, disability, or retirement. When employment was terminated for reasons other than death, disability, or retirement, 35.2% of the companies distributed within one year, 34.5% after a five-year delay, and 25.4% after a delay of between one and five years (a handful of companies used some other approach, so these percentages do not add up to 100%).

---

2. I.e., the participant would wait five full years, and then distributions would begin during the sixth plan year after the plan year in which termination occurred.

Delaying Distributions of Leveraged Shares

Notwithstanding the above rules, the special ESOP rules provide that a leveraged ESOP in a C corporation[3] may delay the commencement of distributions of shares acquired through the loan until the plan year after the plan year in which the ESOP loan is fully repaid. However, the general qualified plan rules may mandate an earlier distribution (see below).

If the company makes distributions in installments, and those installments have been delayed by waiting for the ESOP loan to be repaid, all the installments must be completed by the later of (1) the end of the plan year after the plan year in which the loan is repaid or (2) the date they would be completed if there had been no delay. For example, take a participant who quits in 2014 at age 35. Ordinarily, the ESOP could wait until 2020 (the sixth year after termination) to begin distribution, and then make distributions in installments over a five-year period from 2020 to 2025. However, the participant's vested ESOP benefit consists of shares bought with a loan that is not repaid until 2022. The ESOP can wait until 2023 to commence distributions to this participant, but the ESOP cannot make distributions over a five-year period and delay the final installment until 2028; instead, it must complete them by 2025.[4]

If the distribution is made in a lump sum that has been delayed by waiting for the ESOP loan to be repaid, the distribution must be made no later than during the year after the plan year in which the loan is fully repaid. For example, if the fact pattern in the paragraph above is changed so that the distribution is a lump sum, the ESOP could wait until 2023 to make the distribution, but it could not delay any longer than that.

---

3. It is not clear whether an S corporation can delay distributions of leveraged shares in this manner. As of this writing, some S corporations with ESOPs have done so in the absence of IRS guidance.

4. This example assumes the plan year is the same as the calendar year.

General Qualified Plan Rules

ESOPs are subject not only to the above ESOP-specific rules but also to rules that affect all qualified plans.

Basic Rule

Under Code Section 401(a)(14), unless the participant chooses otherwise, the plan must begin distributing benefits no later than the 60th day after the end of the plan year in which the *latest* of the following events occur: (1) a participant reaches the earlier of age 65 or the plan's normal retirement age; (2) a participant reaches the 10th anniversary of participation in the plan; or (3) a participant terminates his or her service with the employer.[5]

Mandatory Distributions After Age 70½ or Retirement

Under Code Section 401(a)(9)(C), if an employee owns more than 5% of the company, the plan must begin distributing benefits to him or her by April 1 of the calendar year following the calendar year in which the employee attains age 70½. If an employee does not own more than 5% of the company, the plan must begin distributing benefits by April 1 of the calendar year following the later of (1) the calendar year in which the employee attains age 70½ or (2) the calendar year in which the employee retires. (Subsequent payments need to made by December 31 of the year in question.)

---

5. The 60-day requirement poses practical problems for many companies because the ESOP valuation will seldom have been completed by that date, which means that a current valuation would not be available. Because it is generally not possible to meet the 60-day rule, the common practice has been to make a good-faith effort to meet the requirement as soon as possible thereafter. While the IRS has not officially blessed this approach, ESOP professionals report that discussions with IRS officials indicate they will not challenge it.

Distributions After Death

Code Section 401(a)(9)(B) provides that if the participant dies *after* distributions have begun but before they have been completed, the remaining distributions must be given to the participant's beneficiary at least as rapidly as they would have been given to the participant. If the participant dies *before* distributions have begun, either (1) the entire benefit must be distributed within five years after the participant's death, or (2) distributions can be made in installments over the life or the life expectancy of the participant's beneficiary, starting within a year after the participant's death (however, if the beneficiary is the participant's surviving spouse, distributions need not begin until the date on which the participant would have reached age 70½).

How the Special ESOP Rules and Qualified Plan Rules Interact

When the ESOP rules and the general qualified plan rules interact, the rule that would produce an earlier distribution governs. In general, the ESOP rules tend to require distributions to be made earlier, so the interplay of the ESOP rules and the general qualified plan rules usually results in an earlier distribution than would be the case in a non-ESOP plan. For example, suppose that an ESOP's plan year is the calendar year and its normal retirement age is 65. Sally Jones retires in 2014 at age 65, having been in the plan for seven years (since 2007). Under the general qualified plan rules, she could have to wait until 2018, which is the year after the 10th anniversary of her participation in the plan, for distributions to begin. However, the special ESOP rules mandate that her distribution begin in 2015, the plan year following the plan year of her retirement.

Sometimes the general qualified plan rules require an earlier distribution than the ESOP rules would require. For example, suppose again that the ESOP's plan year is the calendar year and its normal retirement age is 65. Fred Smith, who has been in the ESOP for 15 years, quits in 2014 at the age of 64 (and therefore does not qualify for normal retirement). Under the ESOP rules, Fred would potentially have to wait until the sixth year after that (2020) for benefit distribution to begin. In fact, he might even have to wait longer (at least in a C corporation) if in 2020 the ESOP would still be repaying a loan used to buy shares in Fred's account (see "Delaying Distributions of Leveraged Shares" above). However, the general qualified plan rules override the ESOP rules because when Fred reaches age 65 in 2015, the three conditions given above will all have occurred (age 65 or retirement age, 10th anniversary of participation, and termination of service). Therefore, Fred's distribution must start no later than the 60th day of 2016 (i.e., the 60th day after the plan year, 2015, in which the latest of those three events occurred).

Where the Special ESOP Rules Do Not Apply (Pre-1987 Stock)

Because the special ESOP rules in Code Section 409(o) do not apply (unless the plan otherwise provides) to distributions attributable to stock acquired before 1987, the general qualified plan rules control such distributions, which often has the effect of delaying them compared to distributions subject to the special ESOP rules. For example, take an ESOP that did a leveraged buyout of a company in 1986 and never acquired any more stock. The ESOP's normal retirement age is 65, and the plan specifies distributions will not take place before then. In 2003, Ann, a participant who had been in the ESOP since 1986, quit the company at age 40 and hoped to receive her distributions soon. Alas, she is still waiting and, in fact, must wait until 2028 (i.e., the year in which she reaches age 65) to start receiving distributions. Such a distribution would need to commence no later than 60 days after the end of the 2028 plan year. If the ESOP deal took place in 1987, then the special ESOP rules would apply, and Ann would have begun to receive distributions in 2009 instead of having to wait until

2028. Also note that the company could amend its plan to allow pre-retirement distributions.

Distributions While Participants Are Still Employed

An ESOP is primarily a deferred income plan that provides employees with benefits after they terminate employment. However, in certain circumstances, participants may receive benefits from the ESOP while they are still employed:

- As discussed at the end of this chapter, participants may "diversify" their accounts after a certain period and may receive cash or stock directly (however, similarly to the special ESOP distribution rules, companies are not required to offer diversification for stock acquired before 1987).

- The employer may choose to pay dividends directly to participants on company stock allocated to their accounts.

- As noted above, 5%-or-more owners must begin to receive distributions when they reach age 70½.

- There are certain other circumstances in which the plan may provide for in-service distributions, such as after a fixed number of years, upon attainment of a specified age, or due to the participant's financial hardship.

Form of Distributions: Cash or Stock

An ESOP may provide that distributions will be in cash, stock, or a combination of cash and stock. Closely held companies often have concerns about former employees holding company stock, either due to matters such as selling it to third parties or, in S corporations, the possibility of either exceeding the 100-shareholder S corporation limit or having the employee transfer the shares to an ineligible S corporation owner.

ESOP participants generally have the right to demand a distribution in the form of whole shares of stock, with the value of any fractional share paid in cash (even for portions of their ESOP account that were held in cash) and can then sell that stock to anyone, except that the plan may provide that the employer and the ESOP have rights of first refusal to match any offer received from a third party for such stock.

However, if the employer is a closely held company whose charter or bylaws restrict the ownership of all or substantially all (although there is no authority for what constitutes "substantially all," it is generally believed to be at least 85%) of its stock to employees or a qualified plan, or if the employer is an S corporation, the ESOP is not required to distribute stock; instead, it can distribute cash, or the employer can require the employee to sell distributed stock back to the employer.

Buying the Stock Back from Employees

Closely held companies that sponsor an ESOP must provide a "put option" on company stock distributed to participants that allows them to demand that the company repurchase the stock at its current fair market value. (There is one exception: banks and thrifts that are legally restricted from buying back their own securities can avoid providing a put option if their ESOP participants can elect to take their distributions in cash.) At a minimum, the put option must be available during two periods, one for at least 60 days immediately following distribution and one for at least 60 days after the determination of the stock's fair market value during the following plan year.[6] The repurchase obligation (also sometimes referred to as the

---

6. This is the general rule for ESOP qualification under Code Section 409(h)(4). Readers may also encounter references to Treas. Reg. § 54.4975-7(b)(10)-(11) and DOL Reg. 29 CFR § 2550.408b-3(j)-(k), which provide that for stock acquired with an exempt loan, the put option must be exercisable during a 15-month period beginning when the stock is distributed. The 60-day rule

"repurchase liability") that the put option creates is one of the main ongoing considerations in operating an ESOP.

The company may pay for repurchased shares in a single lump sum payment or in up to six annual installment payments over a period not exceeding five years (if adequate security is provided). The company's obligation to make the installment payments should be evidenced by a secured promissory note bearing interest at a reasonable rate. If the ESOP repurchases shares on an installment basis, the company must provide security and guarantee the ESOP's promissory note. Since the company can pay the employee in installment payments over a period of up to five years, selling the stock to the company does not mean the employee will immediately receive the full amount.[7]

For public companies (those whose stock is readily tradable on an established market), there is no put option and no repurchase obligation. If employees of such companies receive stock instead of cash, they can simply sell it on the appropriate stock exchange any time they wish.

Timing Issues and Their Effect on the Amount the Participant Receives

The price the participant receives for his or her shares must always be fair market value, but the way in which distributions are made will affect the amount the participant receives if the company stock price is changing. In each case, the date the shares leave the ESOP is the date as of which the value is determined.

---

under Section 409(h)(4), which was added to the Code in 1978, is generally regarded as having superseded the rule in the regulations, which were adopted in 1977; however, the 15-month rule may be cited by the IRS or DOL (see, e.g., Technical Advice Memorandum 200841042 [June 17, 2008]).

7. A company may use the installment payment method because it allows it to fix the value of the shares at the time of distribution (thus minimizing its repurchase obligation if the share price is expected to rise in future years) while allowing it to avoid paying the entire sum immediately.

- If the participant receives an installment distribution of payments from the ESOP, the amount paid per share will be determined when the distribution is made. Thus, if the stock price is rising, every year the participant will receive more per share for that year's distribution than in the previous year.

- In contrast, if the shares are distributed in a lump sum, repurchased under a put option, and paid for in installments, the price will be determined as of the date of the repurchase, and the participant will receive a series of payments based on the value as of that single date. Thus, if the stock price goes up after the distribution, the participant will not benefit from that rising price because the stock has already been repurchased, and he or she is simply receiving installment payments on that transaction. This can be helpful to the company if its stock is rising in value and it wants to limit its liability for funding stock repurchases.

- Another way for a company with a rising stock price to limit its liability for repurchases is to create a policy that after termination, an employee's ESOP balance is converted into cash, which then is invested prudently until it is paid out to the employee. The amount paid for the shares is determined as of the date the account is converted to cash.

Floor Price Protection

When a company finances a leveraged ESOP transaction by borrowing money, the debt the company has taken on reduces its value. If the ESOP was already in place, then this post-transaction price drop will depress the stock value for participants who leave and receive distributions before the stock value recovers.[8] To guard against this, the company may adopt a floor price protection agreement (also

---

8. With a new ESOP, the stock price will probably recover by the time participants vest, build up their accounts, leave the company, and receive distributions.

called a "floor put") that compensates departing participants for the price drop during a given period, generally by paying them the difference between the price they receive for their shares and the price they would have received but for the leveraged transaction.

Participant Consent; Automatic Rollovers

Code Section 411(a)(11) and the regulations thereunder prohibit distributions being made without the participant's consent when the present value of the participant's benefit exceeds $5,000, unless the participant has reached the later of age 62 or normal retirement age under the plan. The participant must be informed in writing of the right, if any, to defer receipt of the distribution, and must provide written consent only after receiving such information. The consent requirement does not apply to dividend distributions that are deductible under Code Section 404(k) or to distributions after the death of the participant.

A "mandatory" distribution (one made without the participant's consent) of more than $1,000 and not more than $5,000 must be automatically rolled over into an IRA unless the participant elects to have it rolled over to another retirement plan or to receive it directly. If the company does not want to deal with rollovers to IRA accounts without participant consent, it can require participant consent for all distributions or lower the dollar threshold for distributions without participant consent from $5,000 to $1,000.

Employee Taxes

Participants pay no tax on stock allocated to their ESOP accounts until they receive distributions, at which time they are taxed on the distributions. If they are younger than age 59½ (or age 55 if they have terminated employment), they are generally subject not only to applicable taxes but also to the additional 10% excise tax on early distributions from a retirement plan unless they roll the money over to an IRA or to a qualified retirement plan maintained by another company. (The 10% additional tax does not apply to certain situations such as termination of employment due to death or disability, or distributions to an alternate payee under a qualified domestic relations order.) Employees born before 1936 who have participated in the plan for five years are eligible for favorable 10-year income averaging on lump-sum distributions.

If the money *is* rolled over into a traditional (not Roth) IRA or another qualified retirement plan, the employee pays no tax until the money is withdrawn, at which point it is taxed as ordinary income. However, if the person is younger than age 59½ at the time of withdrawal, the rules that generally impose a 10% excise tax on early distributions will apply. If the ESOP distribution is rolled over to a Roth IRA, it is immediately taxed as ordinary income. A distribution from the ESOP is not eligible for rollover if it is one of a series of annual installments over a period of 10 years (or more), if it is a minimum required distribution after attainment of age 70½ (as described above), if it is a distribution made on account of a participant's hardship, or if it is a dividend that is paid directly to plan participants.

The above paragraphs refer to money being rolled over, but if the company is a C corporation and the employee receives stock in an ESOP distribution, he or she can roll the stock over into an IRA if the IRA's trustee will accept it.[9]

When dividends are directly paid to plan participants on the stock allocated to their ESOP accounts, such dividends are fully taxable as ordinary income (not as qualified dividends), although they are exempt from income tax withholding and are not subject to the excise tax that

---

9. An IRA is an ineligible S corporation shareholder, so S corporation shares cannot be held in an IRA on an ongoing basis without disqualifying the company's election to be taxed as an S corporation. However, the IRS has taken the position that an S corporation ESOP can make a direct rollover distribution of stock to an IRA without disqualifying the S corporation election if the ESOP document requires the corporation to immediately repurchase the stock and it does so.

applies to early distributions. However, S corporation distributions paid directly to ESOP participants are apparently subject to the excise tax on early distributions, although the law is presently unclear on this point.

The Net Unrealized Appreciation Strategy

When participants receive a lump-sum distribution of stock due to termination of employment or attainment of age 59½, they are not taxed, unless they so choose, on the net unrealized appreciation (NUA) of the shares—the appreciation in value of the stock while held by the plan, i.e., the difference between the value of the shares when the ESOP acquired them (by either purchase or employer contribution) and the fair market value of the shares when they were distributed. Instead, they pay tax on the NUA later, when they sell the shares. At that time, they are taxed on the NUA at the long-term capital gains rates on the value of the shares when distributed, and at short- or long-term capital gains rates, as appropriate, for any appreciation in value that has occurred since distribution. (If this is the rare case in which employees make after-tax contributions to the plan, NUA is also excluded from income for non-lump sum distributions of stock attributable to the amounts they contributed.) The cost basis of the shares to the plan (or current fair market value, if lower), plus the cash distributed (if any), is taxed as ordinary income when received by the participant (except to the extent of a "rollover" to an IRA or qualified employee benefit plan). If a participant directs the "rollover" of the cash portion of his or her distribution and/or a portion of his or her share distribution, the shares of employer securities actually distributed (and not "rolled over") are eligible for the special NUA tax treatment, but the special NUA tax treatment is not available for any shares of employer securities that are "rolled over" to an IRA or an employee benefit plan.

In contrast, if the entire distribution is rolled over into an IRA (including if stock is put into an IRA and sold while in the IRA), it will be taxed as ordinary income (when withdrawn if it is a traditional

IRA, or when rolled over if it is a Roth IRA). Thus, employees, especially those in high tax brackets, whose ESOP stock accounts include a great deal of NUA may be able to save a considerable amount in taxes by avoiding a rollover and employing the NUA strategy—i.e., avoiding a rollover and taking a lump-sum stock distribution instead to take advantage of lower capital gains taxes.

This strategy is not for everyone, however. First, if the company is closely held (as most ESOP companies are) and the put option period has passed, will the company still buy back the stock without any legal obligation to do so? Second, even with a public company, what if the stock value falls between the date of distribution and the date the participant sells the stock? All the potential tax savings and more could be lost. In the end, the NUA strategy is mainly useful when the stock has greatly appreciated in value (thus increasing the potential tax savings) and either (1) the company is closely held, but the participant exercises the put option and sells the shares upon receiving the distribution or (2) the company is public, and the participant either sells the shares immediately or holds them before selling but is confident that the company's stock value will not fall before he or she sells the shares.

At any rate, the NUA strategy is inapplicable to many ESOP participants because they cannot elect to receive a distribution in shares. For example, this is generally true for participants in S corporations, where the ESOP will typically be drafted to allow only cash distributions (see "Form of Distributions: Cash or Stock" and note 6 above).

Withholding

If a distribution is eligible to be rolled over into an IRA or another qualified retirement plan but the participant does not elect a direct rollover, the company generally must withhold 20% for federal income tax from the distribution. Eligible rollover distributions do not include those, for example, that are paid as a life annuity; paid over a specified period of 10 years or more; payments of dividends directly distributed to participants; paid on account of a participant's hardship; or distributions paid because the participant reaches 70½ and is a 5% owner. Such distributions are subject to 10% federal income tax withholding unless the person receiving the distribution elects otherwise.

Withholding applies only to the immediately taxable portion of the distribution, not to net unrealized appreciation (discussed above). Thus, for a lump-sum distribution in stock and cash, the amount subject to withholding is (1) the amount distributed in cash plus (2) the lower of the ESOP's cost basis in the shares or the shares' current value.

There are exceptions to the withholding rules: (1) the amount withheld must not exceed the amount of cash distributed, so, for example, a distribution in stock is not subject to withholding, and (2) if a distribution consists solely of shares and cash (not in excess of $200) in lieu of a fractional share, no amount is required to be withheld. Also, as noted above, dividends paid directly to participants are not subject to withholding.

Diversification

Under Code Section 401(a)(28)(B), after ESOP participants reach age 55 and have ten years of participation in the plan, they have the right during the following five years to diversify up to a total of 25% of company stock (minus any previously diversified shares) that was acquired by the ESOP after December 31, 1986, and has been allocated to their accounts; during the sixth year, they may diversify up to a total of 50%, minus any previously diversified shares. (For special rules governing combined ESOP-401(k) plans in public companies, see the end of this section.) A participant must be given a 90-day period to decide whether to diversify, and then the ESOP trustee has a further 90 days after the participant's 90-day period expires in which to implement the participant's request.

It is important to note that diversification is cumulative; that is, as a participant diversifies his or her account, the amount available for further diversification is diminished. For example, say that a participant starts off with 1,000 shares in the first year of diversification and diversifies 10%, or 100 shares, leaving 900 shares of company stock. In year two, 100 more shares are allocated to the participant's account, for a total of 1,000 shares. At this time, to compute the 25% available for diversification, the 100 previously diversified shares are added to the 1,000 undiversified shares, for a total of 1,100 shares. The *cumulative* amount available for diversification at this point is 275 shares (25% of 1,100), but the 100 shares previously diversified are subtracted from this, leaving 175 shares (out of the 1,000) that can be diversified.

To satisfy the diversification requirement, the ESOP may offer at least three alternative investments (other than company stock) within the ESOP, offer a transfer to another qualified plan, such as a 401(k) plan, that offers three or more investment alternatives (other than company stock), distribute cash to the participants, or distribute stock to the participants. Remember that in a closely held company, a stock distribution will be subject to the requirement that the company must offer to repurchase the shares at the then-current fair market value. Also, employees who have not attained age 59½ will be subject to the 10% excise tax on early distributions (in addition to regular income tax) if they diversify by taking a distribution of either cash or stock. A participant does not have the right to demand that a diversification distribution be made in the form of company stock (i.e., the ESOP could provide for only cash diversification distributions).

The above requirements (i.e., 25% and then 50% over the course of six years starting at age 55 with ten years in the plan) are the legal minimums: the ESOP plan document may be drafted to allow participants to diversify more than these minimum percentages and/or at a younger age. However, if the ESOP allows participants to diversify beyond the legal minimums, it appears that the "excess" amounts cannot be taken into account when determining whether the diversification requirements have been satisfied (because they are not the mandatory diversifications specified by law). Also, such excess diversifications can accelerate the company's repurchase obligation (due to cashing participants out of their ESOP shares at an earlier age than otherwise would be the case).

There is a de minimis exception to the diversification requirement: IRS Notice 88-56 provides that a participant with $500 or less of company stock in his or her ESOP account does not have to be offered diversification. (If used, this exception should be specified in the plan document.)

Finally, a different set of rules governs a public company ESOP that is combined with a 401(k) plan (a "KSOP").[10] All participants can diversify their own contributions at any time, and participants who have three years of service can diversify all employer contributions. Participants must be allowed to change their investment options; the rules cannot be satisfied by simply making a distribution. These rules went into effect in 2007, and for stock acquired by the plan before 2007, employers were allowed to phase in the new rules over a three-year period beginning in 2007.

---

10. These rules do not apply to stand-alone ESOPs, only to KSOPs.

CHAPTER 8

Choosing Consultants and Trustees

Corey Rosen

One of the questions we at the NCEO are asked most often is "How do I choose consultants to set up my ESOP?" There is no shortage of people claiming to have expertise in this field. All too often, we hear from companies whose advisors told them of their profound understanding of the law, only to find later they were not as expert as they claimed. Choosing well-qualified, experienced people is essential; the penalties for plan disqualification, improper valuations, inadequate repurchase obligation analyses, and other problems can be severe for owners and employees. While there are no formulas for choosing your advisors, there are some key questions to ask.

In picking a consulting team, you will need, at least, a valuation specialist, an attorney to draw up your plan and possibly negotiate with a lender, and a plan administrator. You may also want an independent trustee, an investment banker or financial advisor, and a communications/participation consultant as well. Some people find the best approach is to hire a "packager," someone who can bring together a team of consultants to do each of these tasks. The packager would serve as your primary contact, making life simpler, if more costly. If you go this route, make sure that all of the people the packager is bringing in are experienced and competent.

There also are "turnkey" firms that provide all of the required services except, perhaps, valuation. For this, they usually refer the client to an appraiser with whom they work. We recommend, however, using a completely independent appraiser. The law requires an independent appraisal, and while this has never been specifically defined, we believe an appraiser working as part of a group has too much of a potential bias to provide a price that can help the deal go through. The conflict of interest is even worse, of course, if the appraiser works for the turnkey firm itself. Also, if you hire a turnkey firm, you should make sure that each of the advisors is independently experienced and competent. Ask yourself whether you would hire each of them to be on your ESOP team if they were at different firms. If the answer is "No," then you should not employ that firm.

Choosing a Valuation Consultant

For privately held companies, often the first step in deciding on an employee ownership plan is getting a valuation. If the value of the stock is too low to be acceptable, or too high to be affordable, there may be no reason to proceed further.

ESOP valuation specialists charge widely varying amounts. Part of the difference is the firm's reputation. If your valuation is ever challenged, that reputation may be worth paying for, even if the work performed is the same as that of another firm with a lesser reputation. Another part of the fee difference is how many people at the firm review the appraisal. More reviews may mean more accuracy.

Appraisers also vary in terms of their philosophy toward ESOPs. Different appraisers will place different discounts or premiums on majority or minority stakes, on the presence of a put option (this could increase the marketability and hence the value of shares), on the repurchase obligation (this will reduce share value), and other ESOP-specific factors. Appraisers also vary in the emphasis they place on different valuation methods, such as discounted earnings or comparable companies. You need to tell prospective appraisers what you want to do with your plan, then find out what basic assumptions your appraiser will bring to this potential transaction. There is not a single right or wrong way to arrive at a value, but the different approaches can result in values more or less appropriate to your needs and opportunities.

Finally, you should request a statement from your appraiser indicating whether the firm has ever been challenged on an appraisal and what the results were. The challenge may have been unfair to the company, of course, but you should know about it. You should also know how many ESOP companies the firm has valued.

Choosing a Lawyer

Picking an attorney is somewhat simpler. Like valuation people, however, they differ in philosophy. While this will not have as dramatic an effect as with an appraiser, your attorney should share your approach to ESOPs. For instance, if your attorney believes it is essential to have an independent trustee and only limited employee voting rights, and that union employees should be kept out of the plan, but you think the opposite, you will have to spend a lot of time discussing this. At $400 per hour or more, you could spend your money more productively.

Second, make sure your attorney is providing you with a fee and time schedule that is realistic and comprehensive. An attorney may quote a fee that represents only initial plan design, not all the filings, filing updates, and question answering that will need to be done after the plan is written. Schedules for completion may be hard to predict, but avoid people whose time frame seems unusually optimistic—delays are almost inevitable.

Finally, ask for references from prior clients. If there aren't any, find another attorney. If there are, call a few and find out whether the work was competent, timely, and within estimated charges.

Choosing a Plan Administrator

Much of plan administration is record-keeping, so experience and price can be the key determinants here. Part of your administrator's burden, however, should be to perform and update repurchase obligation studies. Good administrators should have their own data banks of ESOP clients on which to base these studies. Studies that rely on too many assumptions or theories, rather than what actually happens, may be misleading. If you have a 401(k) or other retirement plan, you should hire an administrator who can handle both. This will help prevent inadvertent violations of plan testing rules.

Other Consultants

You may also need separate people to help with investment banking, feasibility studies, communications, or employee participation issues. Investment banking is very expensive, generally charged at a percentage of the financing secured, and is rarely necessary in the typical smaller ESOP. More complex transactions, such as where there is a need to bring in equity investors or mezzanine debt, often do require investment-banking services. The need for other advisors depends on what you can do in-house. If you do decide to hire these people, philosophy is, again, as important as price and experience.

Choosing a Trustee

Selecting a trustee for an ESOP is one of the most important decisions made before a plan is established. Trustees vote and tender ESOP shares (although they may be directed in this by management or employees), oversee the valuation of the stock, are responsible for investment of non-employer securities in the ESOP, pass judgment on the soundness of ESOP purchases, and generally are responsible for operating the plan in the best interests of employees.

There are no legal requirements for who selects the trustee. In most cases, management or the board selects the trustee, but occasionally an employee committee will make the choice; more rarely, outside advisors, investors, or creditors may either choose or approve a trustee.

Anyone can serve as a trustee. Typically, the trustee is either an outside institution with trust experience, most commonly a bank or trust company; an officer of the company; or a trust committee, usually made up of company officers and/or employee representatives.

A directed or "directed" trustee does not act as a fiduciary but rather operates the plan as instructed by the fiduciaries (for example, a bank may serve as a directed trustee that receives instructions from a trust committee at the company). Directed trustees with substantial ESOP experience can provide valuable input and advice to plan fiduciaries (those in the company doing the directing), especially on valuation issues, where they are likely to have considerably more experience with vetting appraisals in detail. Directed trustees do not, however, relieve the fiduciaries of any legal liability. Furthermore, if a directed trustee believes the instructions from the fiduciaries violate ERISA or plan rules, the directed trustee must override the instructions.

Assuming the trustee does act as the fiduciary, having an independent, outside trustee provides some protection should the plan's operations be challenged. Presumably, such a trustee in this circumstance will make an independent decision without the conflict of interest an insider would face. On the other hand, an outside trustee can be very costly (typically tens of thousands of dollars a year, depending on the size of the transaction and the ESOP's assets), and the very independence of the trustee could diminish insider control in critical circumstances.

A reasonable compromise for many companies is to have an inside trustee or trust committee for normal operations but appoint an outside trustee for special circumstances that present strong conflicts of interest, such as an acquisition proposal.

Clearly, the trustee should not be someone without a good working knowledge of the law and the plan. Also, someone who is selling stock to the plan should never act as the sole trustee. The trustee should be negotiating for the best deal for participants, and such a person has an obvious conflict of interest that would be difficult to justify in court.

Where to Start Looking

The NCEO Web site's members-only area provides members with a searchable database of hundreds of fellow members who are service providers in employee stock plans and ownership culture. Certainly, this is a good place to start. The NCEO does not endorse anyone listed, but we do know most of the consultants involved in this field. Using our referral service is preferable to relying on local people who claim expertise; we have heard too many horror stories from people who used this approach. While having people nearby is convenient, location should be a lower priority than other factors. Much of the work can be done on the phone, through the mail, by email, or by fax.

Workshops and conferences are another good place to meet consultants. There are now over 100 ESOP meetings and Webinars annually sponsored by various groups, including an annual conference and other meetings the NCEO holds. They, as well as various publications, are also a good way to become educated before starting your plan. The best way to keep consultant costs down is to personally understand how your plan will work.

Finally, if you are an NCEO member, we can put you in touch with ESOP companies in your area. Their recommendations are usually valuable.

CHAPTER 9

ESOPs, Corporate Performance, and Ownership Culture

Corey Rosen

ESOPs offer a lot of tax and financial planning benefits, but they have often also been touted as a way to improve corporate performance. But do they? And what does a company need to do to make sure this happens?

It may seem obvious that if employees are owners, they will work harder, and if they work harder the company will perform better. What seems obvious is not always true, however. The story turns out to be more complex. ESOPs companies do perform better than would be expected if they did not have an ESOP, but to make that happen, they need to create what we call "an ownership culture." Ownership culture companies do three things:

1. They share enough ownership on a regular basis with employees so that employees see the plan as financially meaningful.

2. They share lots of information. They communicate regularly and effectively with employees to make sure they understand how the ESOP works, usually getting employees involved in the process of communication. They also share a lot of information about how the company is performing financially.

3. They get employees involved in making decisions about how their jobs can be performed better. That takes many forms, such as work teams, ad hoc committees, advisory groups, suggestion systems, and other approaches.

This chapter looks at how we know this and then turns to what we have found are the best practices for achieving it.

The Research

The research on employee ownership and corporate performance comes to a very definite conclusion: the combination of ownership and participative management is a powerful competitive tool. Neither ownership nor participation alone, however, accomplishes very much. The findings also seem to apply primarily to closely held companies. Research indicates that public companies generally do not view employee ownership as much more than another corporate benefit. For this and other reasons explored below, the relationship between employee ownership and corporate performance in public companies is ambiguous.

In 2000, in the largest and most significant study to date on the performance of ESOPs in closely held companies, Douglas Kruse and Joseph Blasi, both of Rutgers University, found that ESOPs increase sales, employment, and sales per employee by about 2.3% to 2.4% per year over what would have been expected absent an ESOP. ESOP companies are also somewhat more likely to still be in business several years later. This is despite (or perhaps because of) the fact that ESOP companies are substantially more likely than comparable companies to offer other retirement benefit plans along with their ESOP. The study was based on comparing ESOP companies to matched non-ESOP companies over the three years before and after the company set up an ESOP. The pre-ESOP period was used to establish a baseline for how the companies that would set up ESOPs performed compared to their competitors before setting up the plan. This difference was subtracted from the post-plan difference to measure the independent effect if the ESOP. So if Joe's Auto Body grew 2% faster than its competitors before an ESOP, the data predict it would grow about 4.5% faster in the post-ESOP period.

While this study showed that ESOPs performed better, it did not attempt to address why that happened. The first study to show a specific causal linkage between employee ownership and corporate performance was by Michael Quarrey and Corey Rosen of the NCEO. That study also looked beneath the results to see what seemed to cause the differences. The study looked at the performance of ESOP companies for five years before and after they set up their plans. The study found that ESOP companies had sales growth rates 3.4% per year higher and employment growth rates 3.8% per year higher in the post-ESOP period than would have been expected based on pre-ESOP performance. When the companies were divided into three groups based on how participatively managed they were, however, only the most participative companies showed a gain. These companies grew 8% to 11% per year faster than they would have been expected to grow without an ESOP, while the middle group showed little change, and the bottom group showed a decline in performance. By participative management, the authors meant a high degree of involvement in decisions affecting everyday work decisions, not employee involvement in board-level or strategic issues. These companies were also very open in communications about financial performance and other company issues.

The results of this study proved out in many subsequent studies, including a large research project by the National Bureau of Economic Research released in 2006 of ESOPs, profit sharing, and other kinds of plans. That study concluded it is the combination of employee involvement in work-level decisions and shared rewards that makes the difference. Participation alone has not been shown to improve performance over the long term. A large number of studies show that the impact of participation absent ownership is short-lived or ambiguous. Ownership seems to provide the cultural glue to keep participation going.

Of course, skeptics argued that this improvement in performance may just occur because employees take lower compensation. That turned out not to be the case, as shown by a 1998 study by researcher Peter Kardas; Jim Keogh of the Washington Department of Community, Trade, and Economic Development; and Adria Scharf of the University of Washington. Their research found that employees are significantly better compensated in ESOP companies than are employees in comparable non-ESOP companies. Using 1995 employment and wage data from the Washington State Employment Security Department, and 1995 data on retirement benefits from a survey of companies and from federal Form 5500, the study matched up 102 ESOP companies with 499 comparison companies matched in terms of industrial classification and employment size. The median hourly wage in the ESOP firms was 5% to 12% higher than the median hourly wage in the comparison companies, depending on the wage level.

In 2010, the NCEO looked at every ESOP company for which data were available compared to other companies with retirement plans. The study found that ESOP companies are more likely to offer a second defined contribution (DC) plan than non-ESOP companies are to offer any DC plan at all (56% compared to 47%). Considering only DC assets originally contributed by the company, ESOP participants have approximately 2.2 times as much in their accounts as participants in comparable non-ESOP companies with DC plans, and 20% more assets overall. The average ESOP company contributed $4,443 per active participant to its ESOP in the most recently available year. In comparison, the average non-ESOP company with a DC plan contributed $2,533 per active participant to its primary plan that year. In other words, on average ESOP companies contributed 75% more to their ESOPs than other companies contributed to their primary DC plan.

ESOP and broad-based equity plan companies are also less likely to lay people off. The 2010 General Social Survey found that 3% of employees with employee stock ownership were laid off in 2009–2010 compared to a 12% rate for employees without employee stock ownership.

Why Ownership Culture Matters

Why doesn't ownership itself matter more? The findings may be easier to understand in the context of what actually happens in a company every day. An employee owner comes to work with a clear financial stake in the company. For some employees, this will increase their commitment. To some extent, just working harder, or more carefully, will make a difference in itself. There will be less waste, customers will be greeted more cheerfully, there will be less turnover, and there may be more actual work done per hour. In most companies, however, all of these things will make only incremental differences to the bottom line. Labor costs are only part of total costs (10% to 50% in most companies), only some workers will actually change their behavior (typically about half, partly because some people are already working as hard as they can), and the total amount of additional "incentive-driven" work that can realistically be expected is relatively small (30 minutes more a day is just 6.7% of total labor costs). In fact, we at the NCEO have done calculations of how much "working harder" alone might save in a number of companies, and typically find the bottom-line impact is only about a 1% increase.

At this point, you might be thinking, "Yes, but the real issue is to get people to work smarter." We'd take it one step further: the real issue is to get whole organizations to work smarter. Organizations work smarter when they use information better. Their people have ideas about how to make their product or service better, less expensive, or both. They create more new products and new markets. They create new ways to organize the flow of work so that fewer people can do more things with the same or less effort. To make a smarter organization, a company needs as many of its people as possible engaged in the task of thinking about how everything the company does can be done better.

In conventional companies, it is up to managers both to generate the information needed to make changes and to come up with the ideas for making improvements. Information moves up and down several layers of the organization, slowing the process of decision-making considerably.

Until recently, this conventional system of management worked acceptably. Companies had the time to develop standardized procedures and keep them in place for years. Information processing and analysis was a slow, complicated job that required special skills. It made sense to organize a company so that these analytical skills were segregated among those able to do the task, while employees were trained to carry out standard procedures developed by others.

That luxury no longer exists. Product life cycles are vastly shorter. Markets are increasingly segmented and specialized and change very quickly. Information can be received, processed, and analyzed by computers in seconds. The sheer volume of information now available is orders of magnitude larger. All this information is also now available in usable formats to many more people than before. The machine operator now knows a lot more about how that machine works than a manager did a decade ago; the customer service representative looking at a screen of information knows more about the customers than managers ever knew just a few years ago. Companies can ignore these changes and plod along, restricting decisions and information to a select group, waiting for management meetings and executive approval to make changes. But they cannot succeed this way. The winners of the next decade will be companies that have more people processing more information and making more decisions faster. These will be the companies that stay ahead of the market or even learn to shape it.

Employees are the best and most abundant source of information. They are often the ones dealing directly with customers, suppliers, machines, technologies, and each other. They have ideas and experiences that can contribute to making the company work better. But in most companies, they are given neither the incentive nor the opportunity to share their knowledge, and managers have neither the training nor the motivation to listen to them even if they do. Employee owners have the motivation, but unless there are regular, clear opportunities to share their knowledge, it is unlikely they will do so.

What does it take to enable an employee to tell another employee or a manager that something should be changed, or that there is something they should know? First, there has to be an opportunity. Do employees even have a time and place to talk to other people? Second, there has to be an expectation that the employee is responsible for sharing ideas and information. Most employees are reluctant to speak up, or even to think in terms of making suggestions, and need a lot of encouragement. Third, management must be willing to listen. Sometimes managers behave as if they are interested but do not act on employee ideas because they feel that would undermine their own position. Fourth, employees need to know that their ideas actually get used, or be told why doing so is not practical.

Just having employees share ideas and information, however, is not enough. Giving people a clear financial understanding of the company will make these efforts even more productive. That is why almost all employee ownership companies now share financial information with employees and many practice "open-book management" or the "Great Game of Business" (an approach developed by employee-owned Springfield ReManufacturing Corporation, now called SRC Holdings). These techniques involve training employees to read detailed financial and performance data and apply this context to the decisions they make every day. Open-book management practices are one of the fastest-growing trends, not just in employee ownership companies but in business generally. As SRC Holdings' CEO Jack Stack puts it, asking people to play the business game without telling them the financials is like asking people to play a game of basketball but not letting them know the score.

Most of the companies that succeed with participation either explicitly or implicitly have a central organizing theme, such as employee participation groups, teams, committees, task forces, cells, electronic systems, training, or financials. These themes help keep people focused and give the process more direction. They are not so pervasive, however, that they restrict companies from implementing participation outside the core concept.

It is important to remember that participation is a process, not a program. While every company has a number of specific things it does, the key to success is not so much the structures used but the commitment to finding ways to create a participation process. Different companies have developed lots of good ideas to create an environment where participation is welcomed. The specific mechanisms ultimately matter less than creating a company where employees feel not only comfortable but also compelled to see that things are done as well as possible.

What Is Participative Management?

Participative management is a term that is often used and even praised but not very well defined. To some people, it just means having an "open door." To others, it means setting up an elaborate decision-making web in a company in which everyone shares decisions about everything affecting them. It does, however, have several key components:

1. Decisions are made by people, individually or as teams, based on their knowledge and involvement in the issue at hand, not on their job titles.

2. There is a bias for getting people to share ideas and information before a decision is made. Often this will be through a meeting of those involved, but other mechanisms, such as e-mail, suggestion/feedback systems, "management by walking around," or even informal networks and conversations are important as well.

3. People are given the financial and performance data needed to make a good decision and the training needed to understand it.

4. Work processes are organized into functional teams (teams of people working in the same area), cross-functional teams (teams assembled from different areas to assess the impact of decisions in one area on another), and ad hoc teams (temporary teams

formed to solve particular problems) whenever the ideas and information of more than one or two people are desirable.

5. Individuals are given as much job responsibility as they can handle, not as little as they need to function.

The emphasis on meetings and teams grows out of the belief (confirmed by research) that groups of people usually make better decisions than individuals. Group participants can bounce ideas off each other, share information, and apply critical thinking to concepts in ways that those same people, tackling the problem alone, cannot. The group dynamic also stimulates an "aha!" effect—the phenomenon of getting an idea that would not have occurred to you otherwise because something someone says stimulates a new thought. Finally, decisions made by groups tend to be more legitimate to group members and, therefore, carried out with more enthusiasm.

While each of these principles is important, it is equally important to define which issues will not be decided in a broadly participative way. These would include those matters deemed too sensitive for group consideration (compensation and firing are two common examples), issues where expertise resides in only one or two people, where there is no time to make a group decision, or, most commonly, everyday issues where decisions are obvious or not important enough to be worth discussing. Participation takes time, and while it usually results in better decisions, better decisions are not always worth the cost of making them (a team is not needed to decide which pencils to buy) or possible to consider (if a customer needs a complaint resolved right away, there shouldn't be a meeting to discuss it). Management should make it as clear as possible just which issues are open for participation and which ones are not, and why.

Formal or Informal Participation?

Participation can be both formal and informal. Informal participation includes the cooperation that often develops among co-workers.

Discussions over coffee or during lunch can be important ways that people influence how things get done. Many supervisors already practice a collaborative style of management, involving many people in tackling problems. The key is developing an atmosphere of cooperation that makes people feel welcome and able to share their ideas with the most appropriate people at the appropriate time. Structures and methods are often a part of the way this comfort level is achieved, but they are only part of the participation process. People with a good idea or important information shouldn't have to wait until the next meeting to share it.

For instance, at ESOP-owned Phelps County Bank, the company set up a variety of innovative formal participation programs early in the ESOP's history. The programs were very successful—so successful that over time, employees found they did not need them any more. When an issue came up, it was just the culture of the company for employees to get a group together and solve it. Management encouraged this and gave great deference to employee solutions. At Web Industries in Massachusetts, employees meet weekly to come up with new ideas. These ideas are periodically gathered together, and then all employees are randomly divided into teams to decide which ideas are the best. The teams then meet to further winnow the ideas to a specific action list for the coming period. As part of the process, employees are given detailed metrics about all aspects of production and performance to help them make the best choices. At Hypertherm in Hanover, NH, an idea generation system results in a few thousand ideas per year (85% of which are implemented) from its 1,200 employees.

These programs work because they provide specific structures— not just permission—for employees to contribute ideas and information. Employees are not accustomed to sharing their ideas and information. Neither school nor work usually prepares people to do this. When employees do have input they want to share, they are often inhibited by a lack of confidence in their way of presenting it, an ambiguity about how or with whom to share it, and an uncertainty about how it will be received. Similarly, supervisors and managers have been trained and rewarded for being able to tell people what to do and getting them to do it. Now, they are being asked to play a very different role. So for companies whose philosophy is only to encourage employees to participate informally, the results are likely to be disappointing.

Formal structures help overcome this inertia by providing a specific format in which participation can occur. There are ground rules for when and how to get involved. There is a chance to observe other people participating to both learn how to do it and overcome fears of doing it at all. Successful programs of this type generate ideas within the formal structure and help overcome barriers to informal, everyday participation as well.

At W.L. Gore Associates, the 10,000-employee manufacturer of Gore-Tex™ fabric and other products, virtually all decisions are made by teams that employees form on a project-by-project basis. Any associate can run with a new idea, without approval from management, provided they can find enough other associates to join their team. Gore operates without reporting systems or much hierarchy of any kind. The philosophy is that authority should follow expertise, not status in a hierarchy. The best way to demonstrate expertise is to be able to persuade enough other people to join a team. Not only has Gore been a stellar performer, it consistently is in the top 10 of *Fortune* magazine's "100 Best Companies to Work for in America" and was named by *Fast Company* as the most innovative company in America.

Giving Employees the Tools to Participate

It is not enough just to let people make more decisions. They need to have enough information to do it well, information about their own job, the company, and the industry. Otherwise, the company runs the risk of having more people make poor decisions.

Sharing financial information is the first step in giving employees the right tools. Without this information, they are much less able to make decisions in the context of what the company really needs. One of the leading examples of sharing information is SRC Holdings (formerly known as Springfield ReManufacturing Corporation) in Springfield, Missouri. An ESOP and management bought the company from International Harvester in 1983, when it had 160 employees and a very uncertain future. Jack Stack, SRC's president, realized that for the company to survive, everyone needed to know the corporate numbers and how to affect them. So a detailed monthly income statement and balance sheet were circulated, and employees were taught to read and understand them. The numbers serve as the basis for small plant-wide meetings at which projections and variances from budget are discussed. Stack says that by providing this information, employees know the score of the "Great Game of Business," as he calls it. Just playing the game motivates people, but it also provides the kind of information they need to help them make better decisions about their own work. A shop-floor worker, for instance, can do the cost accounting on the value of buying a new machine or developing a new product. By 2014, SRC had grown to over 12,000 employees, and its stock value had increased from 10 cents to over $360.

The next step is training and education. Many companies provide extensive educational opportunities for their employee owners to enable them to apply the information they receive. Quad-Graphics, a major printing company in Wisconsin, bought a nearby school to provide all employees with extensive classes on all aspects of printing.

Where Should Decisions Be Made?

Every employee cannot and should not be involved in every decision. Instead, the people most involved in an activity that will be affected, or those experiencing a problem, should be the ones involved. This may mean including people from both the specific functional area (sales representatives, for instance) as well as areas the decision would affect (the people making the product the sales representative are selling). Once the appropriate people are identified, they need to have the resources and authority to involve others when needed to generate the best possible information and ideas.

At Flinchbaugh Engineering (FEI), a mid-sized engineering company in York, PA, an intensive "Kaizen" process engages all employees in involvement. The Kaizen committee meets every two weeks to review suggestions, welcoming ideas for major process improvements and simpler "ah-ha" suggestions, such as moving the company's mailbox. The committee implements the ideas and publishes them. FEI also works on frequent "Kaizen blitz" projects, such as reviewing the company's human resource process in 2007. The process generates hundreds of suggestions per year from almost all employees, most of which are implemented.

This process often involves group decision-making, but just as often it means giving individuals more authority. At Southwest Airlines (which has a profit sharing plan that invests primarily in company stock), employees are empowered to do whatever they deem necessary to make sure customers feel good about the company.

Creating a system in which decisions are made by those with the most knowledge about the issues involved means pushing decisions down lower in the organization than most companies do. It does not mean, however, that managers and supervisors stop making decisions. There are many issues for which they have the best information or perspective to make a decision. In these cases, their authority should be paramount. For instance, imagine that an employee talks to a customer who said that a change in a product would be very attractive. The employee then meets with production people and they determine they could make the change. Finance people determine it would make a profit. But a manager may know that while it would make money, the resources devoted to that use could be better used elsewhere. Only that manager is likely to have the company-wide perspective to make that kind of decision.

Getting Started

Creating a participative culture often requires a great deal of change, and change makes people uncomfortable. Too much change at once will encounter resistance; too little, apathy. It is a difficult balance for companies to achieve, and it requires a great deal of time, energy, and perseverance.

Step 1: Reflect on Goals and Motives

First, think about why you are considering making these changes. If you view "participation" as just another technique, chances are that sooner or later, you and your co-owners will be disenchanted with the results. Employees will see these attempts to get them more "involved" as just another program that will pass. But if you view participation as a permanent commitment to create a more productive and satisfying workplace through sharing information and authority, then you and your co-owners are much more likely to succeed. Making a permanent commitment is essential if people are to make the often difficult adjustments in work styles that participation requires.

The employee response to a non-participative approach to management may be more damaging in an employee ownership company than in a traditional one because of the expectations for greater influence that often develops with ownership. When managers promote ownership to employees to stimulate greater motivation and productivity, they create expectations that need to be fulfilled.

On the other hand, you can take some comfort in the fact that if your motivation is based on a sincere interest in everyone benefiting through opportunities to develop new skills, apply hidden or wasted talents, and find new financial success and satisfaction in working together, then just about anything you do will help, and most people will respond with enthusiasm. Our own research at the NCEO has consistently found that it is the commitment of top managers to treat people as owners, and not particular structures and programs, that matters most.

Step 2: Manager Commitment

For substantial and lasting changes to occur, the company's leadership must be fully committed to creating opportunities for change. Making this commitment visible is a critical step. At Avis, Joseph Vittoria and other top managers spent months touring hundreds of Avis locations to tell people of their commitment to a new way of doing business. (Avis was eventually sold at three times what the ESOP paid for the stock.) In our experience, absent this top management commitment, it is extremely unlikely that an ownership culture can take root from the bottom up.

Step 3: Set Up a Steering Committee

Getting other people involved in the process of planning and creating this change is the first step in demonstrating a commitment to participative management and building on the commitment of others in the organization. A steering committee that includes people from various segments and levels of the company, and, if present, the union, is a good vehicle for this. These committees typically consist of 5 to 20 members. The committee should develop the broad outlines of how to accomplish the transition to a new operational style. Later, it can assess and redirect the program that emerges.

Step 4: Hold Small Group Meetings

You may also want to hold some small group brainstorming sessions about what a participatory company might be. One practical approach is to divide the work force into random groups of about eight people each. The groups are asked to spend 15 to 20 minutes enumerating the obstacles that prevent people from sharing ideas and information more regularly. Then they spend another 5 minutes reaching a consensus on the two or three most important of these. The session leader emphasizes the importance of coming up with specific ideas ("the shifts don't have a way to meet"), not general complaints ("managers don't listen"). The same process is used to come up with two or three good ways to improve sharing ideas and information. Each group designates its own leader and reporter. After the groups finish, the session leader calls on the reporters to list the results. All the results are collated and discussed further.

Step 5: Get Information About Participation

The steering committee should familiarize itself as much as possible with the principles of participatory management. Committee members might read some articles in the business and human resource management magazines that promote this concept. Other employee ownership companies are usually eager to share their ideas, and ESOP conferences abound with panels on the topic. The NCEO's book *Fundamentals of Ownership Culture* provides a detailed look at a variety of techniques, as do various NCEO Webinars.

You may need an assessment of your organization to provide a sense of the overall attitudes and expectations in the company. Spend some time in the steering committee discussing the current level of participation in your company. What opportunity do people have to influence decisions that affect them? How do different people in different parts of the organization see this? Are workers able to influence how their work is structured? Do the managers ask people affected by decisions for their input when they make decisions? Are decisions made cooperatively? When? By whom? What kind of decisions? Consider where and under what conditions participation occurs now and explore ways to strengthen and encourage those practices. This assessment will help you discern where the weak and strong points are in your company. You will then be in a better position to decide how best to develop more participation in ways appropriate to your company. This assessment may be performed through surveys, small group meetings, focus groups, or informally. Some companies hire professional consultants to move the process forward.

Step 6: Planning for a More Formal System

The steering committee can then develop a plan for the formal approach to participative managing. There are many different models of participation from which to choose. Most revolve around a few basic concepts:

1. *Functional teams.* These are small groups of employees within the same work area who meet periodically to review operations and make recommendations to management.

2. *Self-managing teams.* These are the next step up from functional teams. They actually take over all the supervisory tasks previously assigned to a manager or managers, including quality control, scheduling, work assessment, and so on.

3. *Cross-functional teams.* These teams consist of people from different areas who gather to discuss issues where they interact, such as customer service requirements, or company-wide issues, such as safety or leave policy.

4. *Ad-hoc teams.* These are teams assigned to a specific issue. Once the issue is resolved, the team dissolves. Membership usually consists of people appointed by management or the steering committee, plus anyone who wants to volunteer.

5. *Job enhancement.* Individual jobs can often be expanded by giving people more leeway to make decisions.

Creating a participation program involves deciding which combination of these vehicles makes sense for your company. Whatever choices are made, however, it is important to reassess them periodically to make sure they meet current needs.

About the Authors

Scott Rodrick is the director of publishing and information technology at the National Center for Employee Ownership (NCEO). He designed and created the NCEO's present line of publications and is the author or coauthor of several books himself, including the best-selling *An Introduction to ESOPs* (14th ed. 2014). Since 1994, he has created and maintained the NCEO's presence on the Internet. He is an attorney and served at the U.S. Department of Labor as an attorney-advisor before coming to the NCEO.

Corey Rosen is the NCEO's senior staff member and former executive director. He cofounded the NCEO in 1981 after working for five years as a professional staff member in the U.S. Senate, where he helped draft legislation on employee ownership plans. Before that, he taught political science at Ripon College. He is the author or coauthor of many books and over 100 articles on employee ownership, and coauthor (with John Case and Martin Staubus) of *Equity: Why Employee Ownership Is Good for Business* (Harvard Business School Press, 2005). He was the subject of an extensive interview in *Inc.* magazine in August 2000; has appeared frequently on CNN, PBS, NPR, and other network programs; and is regularly quoted in the *Wall Street Journal,* the *New York Times,* and other leading publications. He has a Ph.D. in political science from Cornell University.

About the NCEO

The National Center for Employee Ownership (NCEO) is widely considered to be the leading authority in employee ownership in the U.S. and the world. Established in 1981 as a nonprofit information and membership organization, it now has over 2,500 members, including companies, professionals, unions, government officials, academics, and interested individuals. It is funded entirely through the work it does.

The NCEO's mission is to provide the most objective, reliable information possible about employee ownership at the most affordable price possible. As part of the NCEO's commitment to providing objective information, it does not lobby or provide ongoing consulting services. The NCEO publishes a variety of materials on employee ownership and participation, provides online education, and holds dozens of seminars, Webinars, and conferences on employee ownership annually. The NCEO's work includes extensive contacts with the media, both through articles written for trade and professional publications and through interviews with reporters. It has written or edited several books for outside publishers during the past two decades.

NCEO members receive (1) our bimonthly newsletter on employee ownership issues; (2) access to the members-only area of our Web site; (3) substantial discounts on publications, events, and services; (4) free live Webinars on ESOPs and other topics; and (5) the right to contact us for answers to questions. It costs $90 to join the NCEO for one year ($100 outside the U.S.). To join, see the order form at the end of this section, visit our Web site at www.nceo.org, or telephone us at 510-208-1300.

Selected NCEO Publications

The NCEO offers a variety of publications on employee ownership and participation, such as those below. Most of our titles are available in both print and digital formats. For more information, visit www.nceo.org or call us at 510-208-1300.

Employee Stock Ownership Plans (ESOPs)

- *Understanding ESOPs* is a general overview of the issues involved in establishing and operating an ESOP.

  $25 for NCEO members, $35 for nonmembers

- *Selling Your Business to an ESOP* focuses on the concerns of closely held businesses that are considering an ESOP sale, including the Section 1042 tax-deferred rollover.

  $25 for NCEO members, $35 for nonmembers

- *S Corporation ESOPs* introduces the reader to how ESOPs work and then discusses the legal, valuation, administrative, and other issues associated with S corporation ESOPs.

  $25 for NCEO members, $35 for nonmembers

- *Executive Compensation in ESOP Companies* discusses executive compensation issues, special ESOP considerations, and a survey of executive compensation in ESOP companies.

  $25 for NCEO members, $35 for nonmembers

- *The ESOP Committee Guide* is the definitive guide to creating, developing, and maintaining a successful ESOP committee.

  $25 for NCEO members, $35 for nonmembers

- *The ESOP Company Board Handbook* is a guide for board members in ESOP companies.

  $25 for NCEO members, $35 for nonmembers

- *The Inside ESOP Fiduciary Handbook* provides a basic overview of fiduciary issues, plus an essay on fiduciary insurance, basic ESOP rules for fiduciaries, and sample documents.

  $25 for NCEO members, $35 for nonmembers

- *Don't Do That* is a guide to common mistakes in operating an ESOP and what to do about them.

  $25 for NCEO members, $35 for nonmembers

Equity Compensation Plans

- *The Decision-Maker's Guide to Equity Compensation* explains how equity compensation plans work and what the considerations are for choosing and designing them.

  $25 for NCEO members, $35 for nonmembers

- *Equity Alternatives: Restricted Stock, Performance Awards, Phantom Stock, SARs, and More* is a complete guide, including annotated model plans, to phantom stock, restricted stock, stock appreciation rights, performance awards, and more. A CD with plan documents is included.

  Price: $35 for NCEO members, $50 for nonmembers

- *Equity Compensation for Limited Liability Companies* describes how equity compensation works in an LLC and provides model plan documents.

  $25 for NCEO members, $35 for nonmembers

To join the NCEO as a member or to order any of the publications listed here, use the order form on the following page, use the secure ordering system on our Web site at www.nceo.org, or call us at 510-208-1300. If you join at the same time you order publications, you will receive the members-only publication discounts.

Order Form

To order, fill out this form and mail it with your credit card information or check to the NCEO at 1736 Franklin St., 8th Flr., Oakland, CA 94612; fax it with your credit card information to the NCEO at 510-272-9510; telephone us at 510-208-1300 with your credit card in hand; or order at our Web site, www.nceo.org. If you are not already a member, you can join now to receive member discounts on any publications you order.

Name

Organization

Address

City, State, Zip (Country)

Telephone   Fax   E-mail

Method of Payment: ☐ Check (payable to "NCEO")   ☐ Visa   ☐ M/C   ☐ AMEX

Credit Card Number

Signature   Exp. Date

Checks are accepted only for orders from the U.S. and must be in U.S. currency.

Title	Qty.	Price	Total

Tax: California residents add 9% sales tax (on print publications only, not membership or digital books)	Subtotal $
Shipping: In the U.S., first publication $5, each add'l $1; elsewhere, we charge exact shipping costs to your credit card, plus a $10 handling surcharge; no shipping charges for membership or digital books	Sales Tax $
	Shipping $
Introductory NCEO Membership: $90 for one year ($100 outside the U.S.)	Membership $
	TOTAL DUE $